Daisy Girl Scouts
Leaders' Guide

Revised Edition

Girl Scouts of the U.S.A.
830 Third Avenue
New York, N.Y. 10022

 GIRL SCOUTS OF THE U.S.A.

Betty F. Pilsbury, *President*
Frances Hesselbein, *National Executive Director*

Inquiries related to the *Daisy Girl Scouts Leaders' Guide* should be directed to the Program Group, Girl Scouts of the U.S.A., 830 Third Avenue, New York, N.Y. 10022.

Authors
Candace White Ciraco
Cindy Ford

Contributors
Chris Bergerson
Martha Jo Dennison
Sharon Woods Hussey
Audrey Major

Contents

Special acknowledgements: to many of the councils throughout the country who have been working to serve girls who are five years old or in kindergarten; to the Orange County and Spanish Trails councils, from which many materials in the book have been adopted; to Elizabeth Munz for her piece on disabilities, adapted from *Worlds to Explore: Brownie and Junior Leaders' Guide*; to Corinne Murphy for her work on the World of the Arts; to Janie Wheeler for her direction; to numerous review readers; and to volunteer and staff members who have contributed their ideas and support.

Illustration credits: Uldis Klavins — 7, 18, 47, 50, 57, 64, 67, 76, 79, 89, 101, 123. Richard Lauter — revisions 18, 50, 57; new 84, 117, 121, 125, 126. Kaaren Lewis — 8, 13, 21, 35, 42, 45, 52, 60, 72, 89, 96, 113. Elsie McCorkell — 28, 29, 36, 43, 44, 66, 68, 81, 82, 90, 92, 93, 103, 104, 108, 115, 116, 119. June Otami — 30, 48, 134, 135. GSUSA Archives — 26, 27, 132, 133, 134.

Designer: Keithley and Associates Incorporated

Girl Scouting and You

Welcome to a new and delightful world—discovering for yourself the charm, the fun, the eagerness, the curiosity of five-year-old Daisy Girl Scouts. You, their leader, will introduce them to Girl Scouting. Your enthusiasm, your understanding, your caring, will all make a difference in their lives.

Welcome to a world of discovery—finding out just what and how much five-year-olds can do, why they are special, and how you can help extend their horizons.

Welcome to a wider world for yourself—putting your attributes and skills at the service of Daisy Girl Scouts, reaching out and upward in an all-important leadership role, sharing with other adults who are dedicated to helping girls grow up to be confident, competent, caring adults—just like you!

Daisy Girl Scouts need you. They most especially need you because you

- like children. You enjoy being and working with children.

- are enthusiastic. You have a zest for life and are able to share your enthusiasm with others.

- are curious. You want to learn more about your world and enjoy finding out about people, places, things—life!

- are an alert observer. You take the time to learn as much as you can about all the girls in your troop. You are interested in how they behave and think, in their likes and dislikes, dreams, fears, and joys.

- are receptive to children. You take the time to listen to them, and you care about their needs and their perceptions of their experiences.

- are energetic. Working with Daisy Girl Scouts takes stamina and energy!

- believe in every girl. You have a strong conviction that each girl is a uniquely valuable human being.

- believe in the potential of each girl to contribute. Your work as a Daisy Girl Scout leader helps that potential become a reality.

- understand the traits of your troop's age group. You have taken the time to learn the common characteristics of girls who are Daisy Girl Scout age. You have a good idea of the things they can do and cannot do yet, and how they understand life at this age.

- understand and respect the fact that each girl develops as an individual. Along with knowing the common factors found in girls of similar age, you are aware that each girl grows at her own pace with her own traits and characteristics. As a leader, you recognize the necessity of understanding both group age traits and characteristics and knowing the individual girl.

All the above qualities will help to make Daisy Girl Scouting meaningful, exciting, and fun for the girls—and for you.

Today's girls are exposed to the world outside their homes at an earlier age through preschool programs, television, travel, play groups, and other early childhood experiences. Most girls who are five years old or in kindergarten are ready for Girl Scouting, and being a Daisy Girl Scout gives them opportunities.

- for individual, personal relationships with adults that many children do not have

- to learn about, and believe in, themselves

- to develop awareness of others and a sense of personal responsibility

- to build a sense of personal worth

- to develop an understanding of good citizenship

- for small group involvement

- to learn through play and Girl Scouting's informal education program

- to develop a growing awareness of the world

- for guidance in physical, intellectual, social, emotional, and spiritual growth

Through Girl Scout program, Daisy Girl Scouts expand their world to include adults and children outside their family circle. The Daisy Girl Scouts in your troop may come from different life situations. Some may be the only child in a family and have had little experience with other children; others may have older and younger siblings and be more experienced in interacting with their peers. Some of your girls may come from homes that have the latest electronic devices and games; others may not. Some may have been born or have lived in other countries. Some children may have traveled far beyond their home environment—out of state or out of the country. Others may not have been beyond their own neighborhood.

In Girl Scouting, a girl's growth is based on both her own unique background and the opportunities the movement opens up for her. This book suggests many ways you and your Daisy Girl Scouts can work together joyously and creatively.

Together you stand on the threshold of discovery—you, of the joy it is to work with the girls, and they, of the fascinating world you will help them see. Welcome to Daisy Girl Scouting!

There was a child went forth every day,
And the first object he look'd upon, that object
    he became,
And that object became part of him for the day
    or a certain part of the day,
Or for many years or stretching cycles of years.

—Walt Whitman
"There Was a Child Went Forth"

Characteristics of Daisy Girl Scouts

The Daisy Girl Scout learns by doing! As she acts upon her present environment, she is also gaining a better understanding of her past experiences. Her interest in fantasy has lessened, as her thirst for knowledge about reality has heightened. At this age, reality is magic. The Daisy Girl Scout likes to take on responsibility. She wants to be "grown up" and do things as she sees adults and older children doing them. She loves to share her thoughts and ideas with a caring adult. In short, most five-year-old girls will gain immeasurably from the warm, nurturing atmosphere of Girl Scouting, and in turn will contribute to the group process that is such an important part of the Girl Scout program. When working with a group of children organized by age, it is most important to be aware of the following:

1. A number of common traits or characteristics are found in all children of the same age.

2. Each child must be considered as a unique individual. She has her own growth rate, talents, gifts, personality, intelligence, strengths, and weaknesses.

This chapter describes some of the general developmental characteristics found in children around the world who are five years old or in kindergarten. It gives you a framework—a place to start—for learning about the special behavior patterns, intellectual traits, and emotional nature of girls this age.

Each child in your troop will display some of these general aspects of character, plus all the facets that belong only to her and make her the individual she is. The list of characteristics, then, should be a guide, not a road map. In other words, stay flexible. As in all of Girl Scouting, the needs and interests of the individual girls are most important. As you work with Daisy Girl Scouts, watch what they do, and how and why they do it. Begin to see the world from their point of view. Once you know your girls as individuals, you can plan your actions to meet their needs. For example, if the children seem restless, plan more active (running and playing) games. If children become frustrated at a task, review it to see if they need more encouragement or if the task is truly too difficult. If they have trouble sharing supplies, figure out a way to divide the materials among them. By testing and trying new methods of working with the girls in your troop, you will find ways to help them grow and learn.

Developmental Characteristics of Daisy Girl Scouts

The first of the following two charts presents the specific developmental characteristics of girls who are five years old or in kindergarten grouped into physical, intellectual, emotional, and social traits. The second chart provides, as a reference point, a comparison between the characteristics of five-year-olds and those of six-year-olds.

Characteristics of a Five-Year-Old

Emotional Characteristics	wants to do things herself to bolster her growing independence	wants adult and peer approval and support	understands rules and tries to conform
	is purposeful	can accept direction	**Note:** Daisy Girl Scouts will need time to share experiences and must be encouraged to "take turns." Encourage girls to settle disputes within the group, without adult intervention. If you must step in, try to always be fair and listen.
	is friendly and helpful	is proud of appearance	
	is cooperative	displays some verbal aggressiveness	
	is close to main caregiver, parent	has occasional tantrums	
	is curious about relationships	may be afraid of the dark	
		sometimes blames another for her own mistakes	
Social Characteristics	is developing cooperative play slowly, usually likes to work in small groups of two or three, but will often focus on her own work or play	likes to please adults, is interested in adult reaction and judgments	is capable of compromise, waiting turn, working out disputes with adult support
	has a strong link to mother or main caregiver	likes the family	**Note:** Let the child find a work group in a method most comfortable for her. It is important for the adult to foster the child's relationships.
	is developing ability to play with siblings, especially younger ones	may need support in completing cleanup, in putting away, and being neat	
	likes to play best with peers of own age and others	can engage in group discussions	
		is interested in making up roles	

Characteristics of a Five-Year-Old

Physical Characteristics			
Physical Characteristics	has a good appetite, burns energy rapidly, needs more* frequent snacks	works in cyclic bursts of energy	**Note:** Grasping, pushing, sorting, walking rails, climbing, jumping, skipping, balancing, running, acrobatics, woodworking, taking things apart, tricycle or bike riding, painting, drawing, coloring, cutting, pasting are among the many activities that help Daisy Girl Scouts grow.
	usually tires early in the evening	has better control of large muscles than smaller muscles	
	dreams frequently and vividly	is able to play in one place, but changes positions frequently; usually cannot sit still for long periods of time	
	responsible for toileting, sometimes has "accidents" if she waits too long or is busily involved in something	eye-hand coordination is maturing	
	may still need help with dressing into outer clothes and tying shoes	needs to experience environment through all her senses	
Intellectual Characteristics	is developing language and use of symbols rapidly	can learn and remember the sequence of events in the day's routine	enjoys a sense of competence, socially and intellectually
	questions the whys and wherefores of her surroundings	usually recognizes first name written	cannot easily see the viewpoint of another if it is different from her own
	learns by doing, experiencing, and playing	can print some letters, numbers, words	centers her ideas and her perceptions around herself and how she experiences the world
	needs to play, play, play	can usually count by ones to 20 or more	
	is factual and literal	is not extremely interested in money value	**Example:** On a clear moonlit night, as a young girl walks from one place to another and sees the moon above, she asks, "Mommy, why is the moon following me?"
	can last in an adult-directed activity for about 20 minutes**	can learn her address and phone number	
	is curious, experimental	likes being read to	**Note:** Materials for five-year-olds should be flexible so they can symbolize different things. Good materials are blocks, clay, wood, paint, play house materials, etc. Girls need to have opportunities to recreate their ideas.
	is increasingly realistic	adapts well to school environment	
	likes to collect things	must act/play in her environment in order to develop intellectually	
	senses space and time as here and now, does not have an accurate sense of passage of time	is interested in calendars and clocks	
	may be reading or know letters, words, phrases		

*Comparisons in this chart are with children younger than five.

**However, they can attend to their own special projects for longer periods of time.

15

Working with Daisy Girl Scouts

Although many of the following techniques for working with young children are based on simple common sense, it often helps to have them written down, so you can refer to them now and then.

Build on the strengths of the child. Each girl has her own unique strengths, talents, and gifts. By encouraging her through her strengths, you will help her develop her own potential and grow in positive ways. For example: A shy girl is not socializing, but is very good at doing science activities. Let her be a helper in an experiment where her skills will shine. She can help others and make friends as well.

Build a friendly and understanding relationship with the child. Accept her as she is, feelings and all, so she learns to trust you and your guidance. For example: A girl finds out "she's getting a baby in the family" in a few months and doesn't want one. You accept her feelings and say something like, "Yes, it surely sounds like you're upset about having a baby brother or sister." Let her talk some more about it. As she talks it through, without getting a lecture or adult advice, she will resolve a lot of her own uneasiness and trust you as someone who truly listens and respects her feelings. She may also feel better about getting a new brother or sister.

Be sure that the child understands you. Have her attention when you speak.

Sit down whenever possible. It is important for children to be met at eye level. When you need to work through a problem with a child, stoop down to talk to her.

Use as few words as possible. Speak in simple sentences. Give one direction at a time. Accompany verbal directions with physical help if necessary.

Speak in a quiet, pleasant tone. Talk directly to children, never across the room or play yard.

Phrase directions positively rather than negatively. Example: "Put your cup in the wastebasket, please." Not, "Don't throw your cup on the floor."

Avoid letting a child think there is a choice when there is not one. Choice: Do you want to use the toilet? No choice: It is time to wash your hands.

Be reasonable and timely from the child's point of view. Give plenty of advance warning when an activity is going to end and begin. Small children become confused and frustrated when hurried. Let them finish their activity if at all practical. "It will soon be time to clean up. You need to finish your picture."

When a child dawdles over one phase of a task, suggest the next logical step. Example: "Where is your towel?" when a child continues handwashing too long. Or simply offer her a towel. Such comments recall her to her task, but leave the initiative to her.

Do not hold a child to a uniform standard of performance. Vary the amount of help and support given in a situation according to the child's physical and emotional condition.

Praise the type of behavior you wish continued. Praising a child's desirable behavior emphasizes it, and her undesirable behavior often disappears.

Avoid motivating a girl by making comparisons between her and another child or by encouraging competition.

The overall climate should be that of affection and interest in each child as an individual. Flexibility should be the rule, at all times, and in all activities.

Do not expect every child to enter into all the activities. Watching is a form of participation too. Some children will not be ready to participate in large group activities. Encourage participation, but do not insist upon it. Those who are not interested should be diverted to some quiet activity that will not disturb the group.

Help the children learn to share and take turns. If a child is frustrated about not getting to use the equipment she desires at the moment, suggest a substitute for her to use until the item she wants is free for her to play with. Then direct her to it when it is available. You may have to limit the length of time a girl uses any one piece of equipment if it is in demand.

Be supportive and interested rather than an entertainer for the children.

Always be certain that any discussion you need to have about a girl is not within her hearing or that of any of the other girls.

Allow the child to learn by experience. Encourage her to find things out for herself, but offer help and support when it is necessary to avoid failure or discouragement.

Rejoice with a child when she achieves something important to her—no matter how small. Tell her what you like about what she has done. The more difficult a child is, the more she needs favorable recognition, just for herself as a person, as well as when she accomplishes something.

Intervene only if you are really needed. There will be situations when adult intervention is definitely needed, but the children often will be able to resolve things themselves. Stay close by, but guard against unnecessary interference. However, if you feel the children's safety is endangered in any situation, stop it immediately. Try to foresee trouble and avoid it.

When limits are necessary, they should be clearly defined and consistently maintained. Example: "Balls, not sand, are for throwing." Speak with a parent, consultant, teacher, or director for information about limits they feel are important.

Set a good example. The way you behave, the way you relate to the children and the other adults working with you, will be noticed by the girls and will serve as a model for them.

Use your three basic resources. People, organization, and materials help you build a strong program for your girls. The more diverse your resources, the more interesting a program your troop will enjoy. People resources can be found in many settings. Look for them in your community, through the girls and their families, your neighbors and acquaintances, other Girl Scout volunteers, and council staff.

Local organizations, agencies, and businesses represent resources with a wealth of experiences and information. Many are interesting to visit and explore and often provide free materials. Using written or audiovisual materials can stimulate your activities and ideas. Many libraries lend films, records, filmstrips, and tapes that may be suitable to your troop's interests.

When planning a short trip, be sure to do your homework. Visit the site with the adults going on the trip ahead of time, and check out every aspect the children will be experiencing on the trip. How long does it take to get there? Are there toilet facilities? What type of activities are suitable for the site and for your girls? How will members with disabilities experience the trip, etc.? Visiting a trip site before the girls is invaluable and will help make the experience a safe and successful one.

A buddy system should be used when traveling. Daisy Girl Scouts travel well in twos. They can keep an eye on each other and help you on the trip. Each child picks or is assigned a partner to be with when the troop is walking somewhere, sitting together on a bus, etc. The buddy system is a useful troop management technique. If there is an odd number of children, each girl can take a turn having an adult for a partner.

The four things Daisy Girl Scouts need most from adults are love, acceptance, respect, and approval.

The most important results of your work with Daisy Girl Scouts are the development of:

- respect between you and the girls

- the girls' active interaction with their environment

- a relationship of trust within the troop

You, as leader, should give each child the opportunity to:

- develop a positive self-image

- gain knowledge of her world and how it functions

- share in making the decisions that affect her life

- share perceptions, thoughts, and ideas with others

- play and re-create her experiences and perceptions

- grow socially and develop self-control

Daisy Girl Scouts with Special Needs

As a result of federal legislation passed in 1975, greater numbers of children with disabilities are becoming an important part of public school populations. At the same time, increasing numbers of girls with disabilities want to be part of Girl Scouting, which for many years has considered them valuable members of the movement.

Today one in ten American children has a disability, and Girl Scouts welcome all girls, 5 through 17—including girls with all kinds of special needs. Many of the following ideas about serving these girls can and should be applied to every Girl Scout because they help adults focus on each individual child.

Tips for Working with Girls with Special Needs

Don't hesitate to ask a girl the best way for her to do something. She probably knows.

Offer help in small doses. Girls often need less help than you think.

Understand each child's limitations, special medication, and equipment. Contact the agency dealing with her disability for free information.

Learn to improvise—the more you do it, the easier it becomes. Girl Scout program often becomes richer when it is adapted and personalized

Talk directly to each girl, not through someone else.

Make sure each child is situated comfortably; arrange supplies so they can be easily used.

Prepare ahead of time for new situations—discuss, role-play, and trial-run with girls.

Don't let a girl develop negative feelings about herself. Help her feel she's an important member of the group.

Set the tone with your own attitude; focus on what each girl can do. Your positive attitude will rub off on other people.

Break down each activity into steps for girls. Go over steps in your own mind ahead of time to think through any adaptation that may be necessary.

Make full use of the buddy system when special help is needed. Rotate buddies so everyone gets a chance to know everyone else.

Watch for signs of fatigue. Some children tire more easily.

Involve each girl's parents as much as possible.

Share your successes with other leaders. Ask to observe their troops for tips. Share resources.

Encourage girls to ask and answer questions about disabilities freely.

Set reasonable behavior standards and see that they are met. Having a disability is not an excuse for behaving unacceptably.

Show each girl that you appreciate her for her own sake, not in spite of, or because of, her disability or abilities.

Foster increasing independence as girls show increased ability to handle responsibilities.

Making Activity Adaptations

Each troop personalizes the Girl Scout program in accord with its own needs, interests, abilities, and resources. Whenever adaptations are made, they should be in line with the purpose of the activity. Here are three possible ways to adapt:

Change the method: For example, if an on-site visit is not possible, see a film or have a speaker come to the troop meeting.

Modify the activity: For example, in "Kim's Game" girls are asked to look at objects on a table. After studying the objects, the girls look away from the table or cover their eyes while the game leader removes one of the items from the table. Then the girls look again at the table and try to guess which object was removed. To modify this activity for blind girls, you could ask the girls to touch or smell the objects and try to guess which item was removed from the table.

Substitute an activity that meets the same purpose: If part of an obstacle course requires girls to ride a bicycle or tricycle from point A to point B, girls who are unable to ride could be asked to do another type of physical activity for that part of the obstacle course.

Other Sources of Information

American Foundation for the Blind
15 West 16th Street
New York, N.Y. 10011

Association for Childhood Education International
114 Georgia Avenue
Suite 200
Wheaton, Md. 20902

Child Welfare League of America
440 First Street, N.W.
Washington, D.C. 20001

Children, Inc.
P.O. Box 5381
1000 Westover Road
Richmond, Va. 23220

Children's Defense Fund
122 C Street, N.W.
Washington, D.C. 20001

Council for Basic Education
725 15th Street, N.W.
Washington, D.C. 20005

Council for Exceptional Children
1920 Association Drive
Reston, Va. 22091

Director of Education
Public Affairs Pamphlets
Public Affairs Committee, Inc.
381 Park Avenue South
New York, N.Y. 10016

Education, Training & Research Associates
P.O. Box 1830
Santa Cruz, Calif. 95061

ERIC Clearinghouse on Urban Education
Box 40, Teachers College
Columbia University
525 West 120th Street
New York, N.Y. 10027

Institute for the Achievement of Human Potential
8801 Stenton Avenue
Philadelphia, Pa. 19118

National Association for the Education of Young Children
1834 Connecticut Avenue, N.W.
Washington, D.C. 20009

National Black Child Development Institute
1463 Rhode Island Avenue, N.W.
Washington, D.C. 20005

National Education Association
1201 16th Street, N.W.
Washington, D.C. 20036

The National Easter Seal Society
2023 West Ogden Avenue
Chicago, Ill. 60612

National Information Center for the Handicapped
Box 1492
Washington, D.C. 20013

National Safety Council
Youth Department
44 North Michigan Avenue
Chicago, Ill. 60611

Speech Communication Association
5105 East Backlick Road, No. E
Annandale, Va. 22003

Juliette Low, Girl Scouting's founder, surrounded by girls representing the five age levels of Girl Scouting and wearing uniforms of different periods. They are (clockwise) a Senior Girl Scout of the '50s, a Cadette Girl Scout of the '70s, a Daisy Girl Scout of the '80s, a Junior Girl Scout (formerly called Intermediate) of the '40s, and a Brownie Girl Scout of the '60s.

About Girl Scouting

Girl Scouts of the U.S.A., founded by Juliette Gordon Low in 1912, is part of an international movement united through the World Association of Girl Guides and Girl Scouts. It is a not-for-profit, youth-serving organization chartered by the United States Congress. Based on enduring ethical values, the movement opens opportunities for girls to learn and work, in partnership with adult volunteers.

The Foundation of Girl Scouting

The guiding principles on which Girl Scouts of the U.S.A. is founded are stated in the opening passages of the organization's constitution.

The Promise

On my honor, I will try:
    To serve God and my country,
    To help people at all times,
    And to live by the Girl Scout Law.

The Law

I will do my best:
    to be honest
    to be fair
    to help where I am needed
    to be cheerful
    to be friendly and considerate
    to be a sister to every Girl Scout
    to respect authority
    to use resources wisely
    to protect and improve the world around me
    to show respect for myself and others through my words and actions

Beliefs and Principles

We, the members of Girl Scouts of the United States of America, united by a belief in God and by acceptance of the Girl Scout Promise and Law,

And inspired by the aims of the Founder of the Scout movement, Lord Baden-Powell, and of the Girl Scout movement in the United States, Juliette Low,

Do dedicate ourselves to the purpose of inspiring girls with the highest ideals of character, conduct, patriotism, and service that they may become happy and resourceful citizens.

We believe that the motivating force in Girl Scouting is a spiritual one.

We affirm that the Girl Scout movement shall ever be open to all girls and adults who accept the Girl Scout Promise and Law.

We maintain that the strength of the Girl Scout movement rests in the voluntary leadership of its adult members, in the cooperation and support of the community, and in the affiliation with Girl Guide and Girl Scout movements of other countries through the World Association of Girl Guides and Girl Scouts.

We declare that the democratic way of life and the democratic process shall guide all our activities.

We hold that ultimate responsibility for the Girl Scout movement rests with volunteers.

Girl Scouting's Goals for Girls

The goals of the Girl Scout program are stated in the four program emphases, which sum up the ways each girl can grow through her Girl Scout experiences. The four program emphases are:

Developing self to achieve one's full individual potential: Foster feelings of self-acceptance and unique self-worth; promote perception of self as competent, responsible, and open to new experiences and challenges; encourage personal growth.

Relating to others with increasing understanding, skill, and respect: Help her develop sensitivity to others and respect for their needs, feelings, and rights; promote an understanding and appreciation of individual, cultural, religious, and racial differences; promote the ability to build friendships and working relationships.

Developing values to guide her actions and to provide the foundation for sound decision-making: Help her develop a meaningful set of values and ethics that will guide her actions; foster an ability to make decisions that are consistent with her values and that reflect respect for the rights and needs of others; encourage her to reexamine her ideals as she grows and changes.

Contributing to the improvement of society through the use of her abilities and leadership skills, working in cooperation with others: Develop concern for the well-being of her community and its people; promote an understanding of how the quality of community life affects her own life and the whole of society; encourage her to use her skills to work with others for the benefit of all.

Activities through which girls can achieve these goals are drawn from the five Girl Scout worlds of interest.

The World of Well-Being includes activities that focus on physical and emotional health: nutrition and exercise, interpersonal relationships, the home, safety, work and leisure, consumer awareness. (Look for Suzy Safety throughout this book. She will remind you of important safety factors.)

The World of People includes activities that focus on developing awareness of the various cultures in our society and around the world and on building pride in one's heritage while appreciating and respecting that of others.

The World of Today and Tomorrow includes activities that focus on discovering the how and why of things, on exploring and experimenting with many technologies that touch daily life, on dealing with change, and on looking to future events, roles, and responsibilities.

The World of the Arts includes activities that focus on the whole range of arts—visual, performing, literary—on enjoying and expressing one's self through various art forms, and on appreciating the artistic talents and contributions of others.

The World of the Out-of-Doors includes activities that focus on enjoying and appreciating the out-of-doors, on living in and caring for our natural environment, and on understanding and respecting the interdependence of all living things.

23

Girl Scout Program: An Overview

**Key Aspects of Girl Scouting Fit Together to Form
the Design for Girl Scout Program**

**The Girl Scout Promise and Law:
The Foundation of Girl Scouting**

**The Four Program Emphases:
Our Goals for Girls**

**Five Worlds of Interest:
Activity Areas**

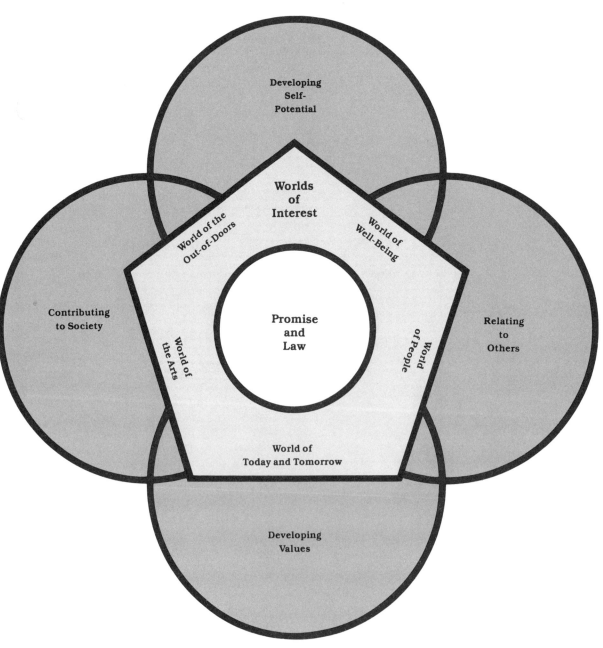

Membership in Girl Scouting

Membership in Girl Scouts of the U.S.A. entitles girls and adults to participate in Girl Scout troop activities and other Girl Scout-sponsored events, to wear the appropriate uniform and insignia, and to be covered by Girl Scout accident insurance. In addition, adult members receive *Girl Scout Leader*, the official GSUSA magazine, and are entitled to receive training, consultation, and ongoing assistance in doing their jobs.

The Daisy Girl Scout pin is the Daisy Girl Scout's membership insignia. It symbolizes the girl's membership in Girl Scouts of the U.S.A.

Active membership as a Girl Scout is granted to any girl who has made the Girl Scout Promise and accepted the Girl Scout Law; is a participating member in the Girl Scout program; has paid annual membership dues; and meets applicable membership standards.

Active membership as a Girl Scout adult is granted to any person who accepts the principles and beliefs as stated in the preamble of the constitution of Girl Scouts of the U.S.A.; has paid annual membership dues; is working in the organization in a defined adult capacity; and meets the applicable membership standard.

Membership Standards

Applicable membership standards are as follows:

GIRL SCOUTS

Daisy	age 5-6	OR in kindergarten or grade 1
Brownie	age 6-7-8	OR in grade 1-2-3
Junior	age 8-9-10-11	OR in grade 3-4-5-6
Cadette	age 11-12-13-14	OR in grade 6-7-8-9
Senior	age 14-15-16-17	OR in grade 9-10-11-12

GIRL SCOUT ADULTS
Minimum age—18 years

Registration

As a leader, you are responsible for registering all girl and adult members of the troop and collecting national membership dues each year. Your Girl Scout council will supply registration forms and instructions for completing them.

If additional members join during the year, be sure to register them promptly so they can receive the full benefits of Girl Scout membership, including the very important activity accident insurance.

Girls or their parents who pay annual membership dues might want to know what the money is used for. The proceeds from annual membership dues go to the national organization, which:

- gathers ideas for what girls want to do in Girl Scouting

- puts these ideas together in a program for all girls

- publishes books that explain the Girl Scout program and supply information girls and leaders need

- publishes *Girl Scout Leader* magazine for the adult membership

- provides technical assistance to councils and leaders via educational opportunities and consultation

- promotes public understanding of, participation in, and support of Girl Scouting

- maintains national centers

The Founder of Girl Scouting

Daisy Girl Scouts are named after the founder of Girl Scouting, Juliette Gordon Low—"Daisy" to her family and friends. She brought Girl Scouting to the United States from England. There she had known Lord Baden-Powell, who created Boy Scouting, and his sister Agnes, who started a similar movement for girls and called it Girl Guides. Juliette Low held the first American Girl Guide meeting at her home in Savannah, Georgia, on March 12, 1912. In 1913, she changed the name of the movement to Girl Scouts and continued to work with great dedication, vision, and strength to bring Girl Scouting to many people.

After her death in 1927, the Juliette Low World Friendship Fund was started to honor her and her commitment to world friendship. The funds are used to help Girl Scouts and Girl Guides travel to other countries, to bring Girl Guides to the United States, and to aid Girl Scouts and Girl Guides around the world.

Juliette Low's life is a model for Girl Scouts, Girl Guides, and people everywhere who want to work actively to make the world a better, friendlier, and more peaceful place. Through the Girl Scout program based on Juliette Low's ideas, girls and adults have great opportunities to understand themselves and others, to develop skills, values, and ethics, and to extend and contribute their special gifts and talents. On page 132, you will find the Juliette Gordon Low story written specially for Daisy Girl Scouts.

Girl Scouting's Special Days

Girl Scouts have three special birthdays to celebrate: October 31, Juliette Low's birthday (also known as Founder's Day); February 22, Thinking Day, the birthday of Lord Robert Baden-Powell, founder of Boy Scouts, and Lady Olave Baden-Powell, the World Chief Guide; and March 12, the birthday of Girl Scouting in the United States of America.

October 31, Juliette Low's Birthday

On Founder's Day, Girl Scouts across the country honor Juliette Low in many ways. You could:

- tell the girls the story of Juliette Low and her life with Girl Scouts.
- teach the girls some Girl Scout and Girl Guide songs and sing them for others at a gathering.
- have a party in her honor and invite a sister troop.
- create and dedicate pieces of art to her: a piece of music, a sculpture, a drawing, a mural or painting—whatever the girls would like to make.

February 22, Thinking Day

The birthday of Lord and Lady Baden-Powell has become a day for Girl Scouts and Girl Guides all over the world to think about each other. You could:

- find someone who knows about Girl Scouting and have her or him visit the girls.
- invite someone from the community who has lived in another country to come and share an activity with the girls. The visitor could organize cooking a dish or learning a dance from the country she or he lived in. There could be storytelling, a discussion about customs, a picture or slide show, etc
- invite an older Girl Scout who has traveled outside the United States, perhaps on a wider opportunity, to share her experiences with the girls.
- talk about the Juliette Low World Friendship Fund.
- plant a tree or shrub in the name of Thinking Day. Send a picture of it to your council office.

March 12, Girl Scout Birthday (Girl Scout Week)

On March 12, 1912, Juliette Low and two other women met with 18 girls to form the first Girl Scout troop in the United States. Girl Scouts celebrate the birthday of this first Girl Scout meeting for an entire week. The week in which March 12 falls is recognized as Girl Scout Week. To celebrate Girl Scout Week, the girls could:

- wear their Girl Scout uniform
- have a Girl Scout birthday party with a sister troop
- act out the story of the first meeting in 1912, imagining how it could have been
- find out if your council plans a theme for each day of Girl Scout Week and plan activities to coincide with their themes

The Girl Scout National Centers

Girl Scouts have two national centers owned and operated by Girl Scouts of the U.S.A. and partially supported by membership dues. They provide opportunities for girls to meet other Girl Scouts from across the country, to explore new environments, and to grow further in their understanding of themselves, others, and the world.

The Juliette Gordon Low Girl Scout National Center

Located in Savannah, Georgia, the Birthplace of Juliette Low is part of the largest National Historic Landmark District in the United States. It is the national Girl Scout public museum, where one can learn about Juliette Low's childhood and her life's work in Girl Scouting.

For more information, write to, Juliette Gordon Low Girl Scout National Center, 142 Bull Street, Savannah, Georgia 31401.

Edith Macy Conference Center

This center is located 35 miles from Manhattan, near the historic Hudson River. It provides an excellent facility for training and educational opportunities for adults. It has facilities for prototype program courses and girl opportunities, and accommodates day tours of traveling troops.

For more information, write to Human Resources, Girl Scouts of the U.S.A., 830 Third Avenue, New York, N.Y. 10022.

The World Centers

The World Association of Girl Guides and Girl Scouts has acquired four world centers, each in a different part of the world. At Our Chalet in Switzerland, Olave Centre in England, Our Cabaña in Mexico, and Sangam in India, Girl Scouts 14 years or older may stay and experience the special opportunities available at each center.

Our Chalet, located in Adelboden, Switzerland, was founded in 1932. A gift to WAGGGS from Blanche Storrow of Boston, Massachusetts, the center is high in the Swiss Alps and focuses on the out-of-doors, with hiking and climbing in the warm months and skiing and other winter sports in the cold months.

Our Ark, the first world centre in London, was established 50 years ago; its successor, Olave House, closed in September 1988. Pax Lodge was built in 1989, the centenary of the birth of Olave Baden-Powell, in whose memory Olave Centre was established.

Our Cabaña was founded in 1957, in Cuernavaca, Mexico. In this city of eternal spring, Girl Guides and Girl Scouts may learn about Mexican culture, customs, and crafts.

Sangam, located in Pune, India, was founded in 1966. Sangam, which means "coming together," is an appropriate name for a center where Eastern and Western cultures meet and Girl Scouts and Girl Guides from all over the world have an opportunity to work together.

Girl Scout Ways

Girl Scouts and Girl Guides worldwide greet each other in the same way and abide by the same motto.

Girl Scout Sign and Handshake

The Girl Scout sign is symbolic of the Promise. The girl holds up her right hand with the first three fingers extended—each finger stands for one part of the Promise—and the little finger held down by the thumb. She makes the sign whenever she says the Promise, at her investiture, and when she gives the Girl Scout handshake. The handshake is given with her left hand while she makes the Girl Scout sign with her right hand.

Girl Scout Motto and Slogan

In the many languages spoken by Girl Guides and Girl Scouts the world over, girls say some version of the motto, "Be Prepared." In this country, Girl Scouts also have their own slogan: "Do a good turn daily."

Girl Scouting at the Five Age Levels

	Daisy	Brownie	Junior	Cadette	Senior
Age or Grade	5-6 years old or in kindergarten or first grade	6-8 years old or in first, second, or third grade	8-11 years old or in third, fourth, fifth, or sixth grade	11-14 years old or in sixth, seventh, eighth, or ninth grade	14-17 years old or in ninth, tenth, eleventh, or twelfth grade
Form of Troop Government	Daisy Girl Scout Circle	Brownie Girl Scout Ring with committee	Patrol system, executive board, or town meeting	Patrol system, executive board, or town meeting	Patrol system, executive board, or town meeting
Recognitions		Brownie Girl Scout Try-Its	Badges (Dabbler, white, green, tan)	Interest Project patches	Interest Project patches
		Bridge to Junior Girl Scouts patch	Signs (Rainbow, Sun, Satellite, World)	Tan badges	Apprentice Trainer's pin
		Dabbler badge while bridging	Junior Aide patch	Leader-in-Training pin	Leader-in-Training pin
			Bridge to Cadette Girl Scouts patch	Counselor-in-Training pin	Counselor-in-Training pin
				From Dreams to Reality patch	Career Exploration pin
				Service Training bars	Service Training bars
Basic Resources	Daisy Girl Scouts Leaders' Guide	Brownie Girl Scout Handbook*	Junior Girl Scout Handbook*	Religious recognitions	Religious recognitions
		More Brownie Girl Scout Try-Its	Girl Scout Badges and Signs*	American Indian Youth Certificate and Award	American Indian Youth Certificate and Award
		Cadette and Senior Girl Scout Handbook*		Cadette Girl Scout Challenge pin	Senior Girl Scout Challenge pin
		Cadette and Senior Girl Scout Interest Projects		Cadette Girl Scout Leadership Award	Senior Girl Scout Leadership Award
		From Dreams to Reality: Career Cards			
Supplementary Resources	The Wide World of Girl Guiding and Girl Scouting*			Girl Scout Silver Award	Ten-Year Award
				Bridge to Senior Girl Scouts patch	Girl Scout Gold Award
	Other young childhood publications in Girl Scout publications catalog				Bridge to Adults Girl Scouts pin

*A separate leaders' guide is available for each of these publications.

Girl Scouting at the Five Age Levels

The goals, principles, and beliefs of Girl Scouting, as they have been outlined in this chapter, are basic to all age levels. The particulars of Girl Scout program, however, change to meet the needs and interests of the girls in each age group. The chart on the previous page summarizes these adaptations, indicating the progression from Daisy Girl Scouts to Senior Girl Scouts. The next chapter will deal with Girl Scout program as it applies specifically to Daisy Girl Scouts.

Girl Scout Program for Daisy Girl Scouts

Girl Scouting's aim for each Daisy Girl Scout is that she will grow, as her older sisters do in Brownie, Junior, Cadette, and Senior Girl Scouts. Through activities based on the five worlds, she will expand her own world as she progresses toward the goals stated in the program emphases. But she will do it at her own pace and in her own way. That is why Girl Scout program for Daisy Girl Scouts is designed just for them and why their activities are different from those that occur at any other age level.

The Daisy Girl Scout Circle

"...the democratic process shall guide
all our activities."
—Girl Scout beliefs and principles

The Daisy Girl Scout's introduction to troop government comes in the Daisy Girl Scout circle. This is where she learns the formal group decision-making process that is such an important part of Girl Scouting. In the circle, you play an active role in stimulating discussion and helping plan activities. It meets once a month, or less frequently, to plan for future activities and solve problems.

The circle should not be longer than 15 minutes and should not take the place of, or be confused with, the sharing time that happens at every meeting.

Sharing time should be initiated by the girls themselves while you only offer guidance. The Daisy Girl Scout circle, on the other hand, should be initiated and directed by you. In both instances, the girls

should be permitted to express their views without censure. Girls can be made aware of the difference between sharing time and a Daisy Girl Scout circle. Once they understand, they can confine their discussion in a circle to the business at hand.

Planning Your Daisy Girl Scout Year

In Daisy Girl Scouts, you will prepare an overall plan for the year. Though this general plan is based on consultation with your troop committee and Girl Scout resource people, you will decide on specific troop activities with the girls. Thus, Daisy Girl Scouts gain the experience of planning by making a series of small decisions. Each specific activity should be chosen from only two or three alternatives. Five-year-olds may have difficulty making choices from a larger number of options.

Planning with Your Troop Committee

You will meet with Girl Scout resource people and your troop committee to:

- make a year plan based on developmental and interest level of the children. Family members of girls should be encouraged to get involved with the troop in whatever capacity they are available. Parents and other relatives may have many excellent ideas and resources at their fingertips. The more that families are constructively involved in Daisy Girl Scouting, the more meaningful will be the troop's experiences.

33

- identify where additional assistance is needed. This could be in arranging transportation, in locating consultants, or in obtaining required permissions. Be sure to check *Safety-Wise* for precautions and planning tips.

- identify aspects of planning that will be left to the girls. Prepare alternate activity ideas.

A sample three-month plan prepared by you and your troop committee might look something like this:

Possible activities for October

Visit a cider mill

Make apple sauce

Visit folk art exhibit showing pioneer crafts

Halloween party

Juliette Low birthday party

Possible Activities for November

Service project for Thanksgiving

Make bread

Make gifts for family

Try some Today and Tomorrow activities

Visit a Brownie Girl Scout troop

Possible Activities for December

Make cards

Learn about special days in many cultures and religious groups — Christmas, Hanukkah, Kwanza, etc.

Attend outdoor event with Brownie Girl Scout troop

Planning with Your Troop

After you have worked out a tentative year plan with your troop committee, you will work with the girls in a Daisy Girl Scout circle to decide about specific activities.

When planning, you should take into consideration the Girl Scout special days, American national holidays, and the various cultural and religious holidays celebrated by the girls in your troop.

A sample of the final month-by-month plan decided upon by you and the girls might look something like this:

October

Make apple sauce

Visit cider mill

Have Juliette Low birthday party

One meeting for business, with just-for-fun activities decided that day

November

Help in a Brownie Girl Scout troop service project

Brownie-Daisy Girl Scout planning meeting

Make plaster of paris

Make hand print paperweights

Paint and decorate paperweights

December

Learn about special celebrations around the world

Visit a house of worship and hear about the people's holidays

Plan an outdoor event with another troop

Managing Your Daisy Girl Scout Troop

> "...to serve God and my country, to help people at all times, and to live by the Girl Scout Law..."
> —Girl Scout Promise

Each meeting of Daisy Girl Scouts should be from 40 to 60 minutes long, depending on the needs and interests of the girls.

Below is a sample meeting plan that follows a general meeting format. As with all Girl Scout activities, you should remain flexible, making changes and adaptations to meet the needs and interests of the girls. The schedule of the sample meeting is approximate. Some meetings may need more time for an activity, some an extended sharing time, some a shorter closing, etc. Flexibility, wise planning, and observation of how things are going will help you judge the proper timing of a meeting.

Activity	Time
Opening	5 minutes
Song and Promise	
Sharing time	10 minutes
Daisy Girl Scout circle (once a month)	10 minutes
Program activity	20 minutes
Clean-up	10 minutes
Closing	5 minutes

Each meeting should begin with a short opening ceremony that might include a song, the Promise, and the flag ceremony. You should plan the opening, until the girls are comfortable with this process. By the latter part of the year, they should be able to plan and carry out opening and closing ceremonies.

The opening is followed by a sharing time where girls are given an opportunity to talk about the events of the day or the past week. This sharing time should have a specific beginning and ending, which you determine. Five-year-olds love to talk so much that half the meeting can be spent in discussion if you allow it. In fact, if the girls do have a great deal to discuss, a large part of the meeting time is well spent in sharing. Use your discretion and let the needs of the girls be your guide. Sharing time should occur at every meeting, and remember to keep it separate from the Daisy Girl Scout circle.

Since Daisy Girl Scouts are usually able to handle well-defined responsibilities without assistance, jobs within the troop can be rotated on a week-to-week basis. Officers are not elected in Daisy Girl Scout troops. However, girls may take turns doing various tasks—recording attendance, helping with cleanup, etc. A kaper chart is useful for identifying and recording jobs and keeping track of who is responsible for their completion.

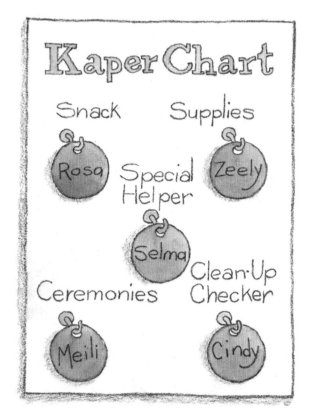

Program activities should be in keeping with the developmental level of the girls. Whenever possible, projects should be completed in one troop meeting. Parents should be informed of program activities and should feel comfortable in making judgments as to the appropriateness of any activity for their child.

It is amazing how long five-year-olds can remain at a task they enjoy and have interest in, and equally amazing how short their attention span can be if they are not interested in an activity. This is a characteristic of this age level, and should not be viewed as negative. The most important thing is to remember to stay flexible and allow the children to move at their own speed.

The following activities can be adapted to fit the needs and interests of the girls in your troop.

Activity Suggestions

Opening Songs: The girls can sing "Make New Friends," "Whene'er You Make a Promise," etc.

Girl Scout Promise and Law: You recite the Promise and Law, discuss it, and have girls act out the meaning.

or

The girls suggest what the Girl Scout Promise means to them.

or

The girls draw pictures showing ways they can serve God, their country, and mankind.

Sharing time: When members of the troop discuss their day, their week, their concerns, etc.

or

Have a silent discussion, with girls acting out or drawing an experience from the previous week.

Daisy Girl Scout circle: You and the girls plan future activities (meeting once a month).

Program activity: This may be a trip, game, art project, a story, or a dramatics project, a visit by a consultant, etc. The length of the meeting will be determined by the type of activity planned.

Cleanup: Tasks should be assigned on a rotating basis and recorded on a kaper chart.

Helping Daisy Girl Scouting Happen

There are many sources of support for you and your Daisy Girl Scouts. Help can come from a variety of places, in a number of ways, and from many people. You cannot, and should not, carry the entire responsibility. Following are groups and individuals that you can call upon for support.

Leadership Team

The leadership team is composed of you and your assistant leader and/or program aides. The ratio of girls to adults for Daisy Girl Scout troops is five to one. Members of your leadership team might include adults or Cadette and/or Senior Girl Scouts. All members of your team must complete the appropriate training to work with Daisy Girl Scouts.

Cadettes who are 14 and Senior Girl Scouts, who assume leadership roles in your troop, also must conform to the council policies and standards that apply to them. Girls may use their leadership team responsibilities as part of the requirements for Challenges, interest projects, or leadership awards.

In addition to the members of the leadership team, who plan and carry out activities with the girls in the troop, a host of other adults and/or groups may work with you and your team in support of troop program and of your troop itself. Depending on your local resources, these include any or all of the following.

The Service Team

The service team is that group of people who provide direct services to troops within a neighborhood or other geographic subdivision of the council. They are responsible for seeing that troops are available to every girl who wants to become a Girl Scout (troop organizers), for providing ongoing help and advice to each troop leader (troop consultants), and for giving other special assistance when needed.

One member of the service team is assigned to work with you and your troop. It is her job to see that your leadership team receives the services needed to deliver quality Girl Scout program to the girls in your troop. Turn to her with your questions, concerns, and needs. If she cannot help you, she will see you get the assistance you need. She will also introduce you to the many other human and material resources available to you—program consultants, publications, handbooks, training courses, etc.

The Troop Committee

A troop committee is the adult network that gives support to the troop. It is comprised of from three to seven women and/or men who provide the troop with whatever special help it needs.

You, as the leader, will appoint the troop committee. (There are times when the troop committee is organized prior to the selection and placement of the leader, but this does not affect the leader's responsibility for it.) The member of the service team assigned to you will work with you on the recruitment, selection, and training of the troop committee chairman and members.

Forming a troop committee divides the work of managing the troop among the members of the group, so the entire responsibility for the troop is not left to one or two people. The committee will be accountable to you for giving support to the troop. Thus, your time, energy, and expertise can be applied directly to working with the girls.

Here are some ways a troop committee can help you and your troop:

- aid in the development and implementation of your ideas

- ensure continuity of program for a troop that is temporarily without a leader

- keep you informed of the needs, resources, and viewpoints of the community

- secure community backing for your troop

- tell friends and other groups about Girl Scouting

- share its expertise, special interests, or hobbies with your troop

- assist your leadership team with troop registration and other troop management responsibilities or tasks

In recruiting troop committee members, you will want to consider people with knowledge of the community, its people, and its resources. Individuals with enthusiasm and the ability to interest and involve other parents and community leaders in actively supporting the troop are invaluable on a troop committee. Parents, professional and career people, retirees, grandparents, and former Girl Scout adult volunteers are likely candidates for troop committee appointment.

If your troop is sponsored, the sponsoring group usually appoints someone to be a liaison on your troop committee. Consider asking the teacher of a kindergarten class to serve on the troop committee. This way you will know what the girls are doing in school and can plan troop activities that complement, not duplicate, their schoolwork.

Daisy Girl Scout Families

This essential support group includes parents, guardians, fathers, mothers, foster parents, grandparents, older brothers and sisters, aunts and uncles. Each girl's family is a potential resource of great value for the troop, but planning for, and making use of, parent and family support takes time. You need to know the parents' expectations for their children. They need to know about Girl Scouting, its goals for Daisy Girl Scouts, the kinds of activities the girls will be involved in, and the kind of help they can offer. Parents should be assured you care about their children's development and welcome their suggestions and their participation in whatever capacity they are available. See page 40 for a "Guide to Family Support."

The Sponsoring Organization

Your Girl Scout council may enter into an association with a community organization or business that agrees to sponsor your troop. The sponsor's aims and objectives will be compatible with those of Girl Scouting. Schools, religious groups, PTAs, men's and women's service groups, professional and fraternal societies, civic organizations, and labor groups are examples of community groups that give support to a troop like yours.

The specific responsibilities of your sponsor and your Girl Scout council would be described in a written agreement between them.

Your sponsor might assume responsibility for some or all of the following:

- appointing a liaison member to serve on troop committee
- publicizing Girl Scouting
- providing resources and services for your troop: books, flags, art supplies, and other materials, transportation, adult training, etc.
- providing meeting places
- providing appropriate financial assistance to the troop

In turn, your Girl Scout troop would:

- keep your sponsor informed of troop activities
- include your sponsor in appropriate activities
- recognize and publicize your sponsor's contribution to the stability of the troop
- actively seek opportunities to provide services to your sponsor
- make membership available to your sponsor

Every Girl Scout council establishes its policy on sponsorship. If your troop is sponsored, the service team member assigned to work with you will assist you in establishing and maintaining relationships with the troop's sponsoring group.

Girl Scout Council

In addition to the various support resources described above, you and the troop receive many additional services from your Girl Scout council. Your council can provide:

- outdoor resources and facilities
- councilwide activities and projects
- opportunities for adult learning and sharing
- access to Girl Scout and other books, films, and resources
- interpretation of the council organization and operation
- opportunities for you to express needs and make suggestions
- interpretation and clarification of national and local policies, standards, and procedures
- feedback on how well you are doing your job

These services are provided by the service team in your area of the council, the team member assigned to you, and other council personnel. There are many people behind you to help you work with the girls in your troop, and to make your job as a Daisy Girl Scout leader rewarding.

A Guide to Family Support

You will find the time it takes to involve the families of your girls well spent. By inviting their participation in the troop's activities, you will be offering the girls exposure to a network of experienced, sympathetic adults.

The Parents' Meeting

One of the most important means of gaining and channeling family support is a parents' meeting held at the beginning of the Girl Scout year. When selecting the time for this event, the working schedules of mothers and fathers should be considered, since it is important that as many parents or other family members as possible attend. The meeting provides an opportunity for you to:

- organize the troop and troop committee

- get acquainted with the parents and other family members

- learn about their expectations for their daughters' Girl Scout experience

- explain the overall aspects of Girl Scout program

- talk about the girls' interests and plans for the year

- show families how they can help

- collect registration money and gather information

GETTING STARTED

It is important to organize the meeting so that everything runs smoothly. To begin, contact the neighborhood chairman and ask her to arrange for a member of the service team to help you plan and conduct a parents' meeting.

Consider who will be invited. Are girls to be included (parents are more likely to attend if they are)? If so, are activities planned for them?

Arrange for a meeting place and time, giving careful consideration to the time schedules of working parents.

Line up any audiovisual equipment needed and make sure it's in good working order.

Check on your supplies: masking tape and large sheets of paper, felt-tip pens, name tags and pins to attach to them, attendance sheets, and any handouts for parents.

Plan the refreshments.

Notify parents by mail, phone, or notes sent home with the girls.

ON THE DAY OF THE MEETING

Once the families have gathered, welcome them. It's important not only to let the families get to know you and one another, but also to tell them how to contact you in the future.

Tell the Girl Scout story, either through a short talk, a filmstrip, or slides, or have girls and parents who have been previously involved in Girl Scouting give a brief presentation. In any case, make sure to cover the purpose of the Girl Scout program and activities, the benefits girls will derive from Girl Scouting, the Promise and Law, investiture and rededication, the program framework for this troop's age level, the name of the council and location of the council office, and an explanation of the volunteer organization.

Next, talk about the finances: membership dues, program and field trip money, and the cost of uniforms and materials.

Then discuss the health and safety standards the organization observes and explain the need for parent consent forms and permission slips.

Talk about your troop's activities—when and where meetings are held and what special events, field trips, and outdoor expeditions may be in store.

After you've explained the troop's hopes and plans for the year, it is a good time to ask for a commitment from family members to support the troop. Circulate a list of areas needing support and encourage fathers, mothers, and other relatives to volunteer their talents as resource persons or troop committee members.

Finally, thank the parents for attending and tell them the ways that you will be keeping in touch with them throughout the rest of the year.

Following the meeting, you or someone from your service team or troop committee should arrange to contact parents who were unable to attend.

Other Ways to Involve Families

By continuing to communicate your troop's plans and needs to the girls' families, you are more likely to get the help the girls need to carry out their plans. You may want to use some of the following ways to keep families in touch with your troop throughout the year.

Troop newsletters: A newsletter on what the troop is doing could be written with the help of the girls or by a troop committee member.

Parent newsletters: This means of addressing the family directly could take the form of a special newsletter developed by the council, a family bulletin, or an insert or regular column in the council bulletin.

Workshops and seminars: You might suggest that your council sponsor training events parents would want to attend, either alone or with their daughters—for example, children's television viewing, use of computers, money management, first aid, parent effectiveness training, smokers' clinics, cardiopulmonary resuscitation, etc.

Outdoor activities: Family members may be invited to your troop cookouts, picnics, hikes, or family camping weekends. These outdoor activities may be either troop-sponsored or neighborhood events.

Troop activities: Families also may be asked to attend investitures, bridging activities, fashion shows, covered-dish dinners, field trips, sports events, and intertroop activities.

Parent assistance: Asking a parent for assistance with a specific activity is often the key to family involvement.

Program Standards for Daisy Girl Scouts

The following program standards have been developed specifically for Daisy Girl Scouting. (See *Safety-Wise* for complete information.)

Adult Leadership

Each Daisy Girl Scout troop should have one adult leader and at least one assistant leader. The ratio of adults to girls in troops is one adult to every one to five Daisy Girl Scouts.

At least two adults should accompany a troop when they are on field trips or attending an event. One or more additional adults may be needed, depending on the size of the troop. The ratio of adults to girls for field trips or events, is two adults for the first five Daisy Girl Scouts and one adult to each additional three girls.

Under the leadership of the troop leader, and with parents, guardians, or other family members, a Daisy Girl Scout troop may participate in occasional overnight family camping experiences.

Troop Organization

Troops should meet often enough to fulfill the needs and interests of girls and to maintain continuity. Daisy Girl Scouts usually meet once a week for 40 to 60 minutes.

Activities Involving Money

Daisy Girl Scouts should not be involved in handling any money, including troop dues; in troop money-earning activities; in council-sponsored product sales; or in other types of fund raising. Daisy Girl Scouts may not sell cookies or other products. Adults are responsible for meeting the modest cost of troop activities.

Troop Funds

Service team members, parents, field directors, and sponsors will provide ideas to develop modest troop funds. You and your troop committee may also meet to decide on appropriate methods of developing troop funds. For example, parents could pay modest monthly activity fees based on an estimated annual troop budget. Councils may raise additional monies for Daisy Girl Scouting. Sponsors may want to subsidize a troop.

Uniforms

Daisy Girl Scouts are encouraged but not required to wear their uniforms—to meetings, public ceremonies, or events; in synagogues, churches, or temples; on Girl Scout Sunday or Sabbath; when traveling as Girl Scouts; or when serving their communities.

Girl Scout adults also are encouraged but not required to wear uniforms. If you do not wear a uniform, the Girl Scout pin and World Association pin may be worn to meetings and other Girl Scout events.

See *Girl Scout Uniforms, Insignia, and Recognitions* for more details on the proper way to wear the adult uniform and where to wear the insignia.

Ready-made uniforms and, for those interested in making their own, uniform kits are available for adults and all Girl Scout age levels.

The Daisy Girl Scout Scrapbook

An enjoyable ongoing activity for Daisy Girl Scouts is making a scrapbook. They can staple or sew together with yarn several pieces of sturdy construction paper and decorate the covers. Or they can bring a ready-made scrapbook.

When girls receive their Daisy Girl Scout certificates, they can attach or paste them in their scrapbooks. Then, throughout the year, girls can build a collection of mementos of their experiences as Daisy Girl Scouts.

They might start with a picture of themselves and then ask you or someone at home to write in their names, troop number, your name, and names of the troop members. They might even add their thumbprints to these personal records. They can cut out or draw pictures of ways they are prepared to help people. They can add the dates of their birthdays and how old they are. They can draw or find pictures of the things they do as Daisy Girl Scouts, and paste in the things they find on outings or make in meetings.

The scrapbooks may be started at a troop meeting and continued at home, or they can be left at the meeting place to be used when the girls want to add to them.

When Daisy Girl Scouts work on the scrapbooks at home, parents become more involved in what the girls are doing. Home may also be a safer place for girls to keep the book. Throughout the year, girls can bring in their scrapbooks to show each other and share again the good times they've had in Daisy Girl Scouts.

Daisy Girl Scout Certificates

In the beginning of the year, each girl may receive the Daisy Girl Scouts Beginning Certificate. It welcomes her to Daisy Girl Scouting and may be placed in the front of her scrapbook. The investiture ceremony is probably the best time to give the certificates to the girls.

At the end of the year, girls may receive the Daisy Girl Scouts Ending Certificate, which can be placed on the last page of her scrapbook. You can give this to each girl at the bridging ceremony, or you may want to plan a separate celebration for this prior to the bridging to Brownie Girl Scouts ceremony.

Recognitions

At the older age levels, recognitions are objects that symbolize a girl's accomplishments in Girl Scouting, but Daisy Girl Scouts do not earn this type of recognition.

Giving object recognitions to girls this age encourages them to focus on the object rather than to be part of the process. They can become so preoccupied with the actual collecting that the meaning of

their experiences becomes secondary. Daisy Girl Scouts do not yet understand that it is not the object itself but what it represents that is important. It is therefore quite possible to foster a non-learning atmosphere in which those who have the most or prettiest object recognitions will be considered the "best" by their peers. It must be remembered that it is through her experiences, through the process itself, that the Daisy Girl Scout develops self-knowledge and confidence and begins to learn about the world around her.

Daisy Girl Scouts do have their own kind of recognition. The uniform, the certificates that are given at the beginning and end of the Daisy Girl Scout year, the scrapbook, and the welcoming, investiture, bridging, and other ceremonies provide the girls with appropriate, meaningful symbols they can understand. The insignia and acknowledgement from you and their sister troop members provide both formal and informal recognition of them as Daisy Girl Scouts. The most important and valid rewards for girls this age are those gained in an atmosphere where they have support, care, success in worthwhile learning experiences, and encouragement and praise from their peers and the adults working with them.

Daisy Girl Scout Ceremonies

In Daisy Girl Scouting, ceremonies may be held throughout the year. A troop may choose to celebrate a birthday, a special day, or an event whenever they choose. Formal ceremonies can honor times of transition, such as entering Girl Scouting or bridging to Brownies. Simple ceremonies often begin or end meetings. The most important aspects of ceremonies for Daisy Girl Scouts are simplicity, appropriateness, clarity, and meaning. With understanding guidance, Daisy Girl Scouts will be able to share ideas in order to plan many of their own ceremonies.

Often, the most meaningful ceremonies are these that the girls create and plan themselves. In

Girl Scout Promise

On my honor, I will try:
to serve God and my country,
to help people at all times,
And to live by the Girl Scout Law.

the beginning, however, you will have to suggest ideas to the girls and go through some of the ceremonies with them.

Opening and Closing Ceremonies

Each Daisy Girl Scout meeting should have a definite opening and closing. Children enjoy repetition, and opening and closing ceremonies offer them the comforting feeling of having "traditions" at the meeting and knowing what to expect.

Many times, the opening and closing ceremonies can be the same thing. For example, a meeting could begin with everyone joining hands in a circle, singing a song or calling their names—"Kim's here," "Henrietta's here," etc. When the meeting ends, the same circle could be formed with everyone singing a song or saying "Goodbye, see you next week," to one another.

These are other ideas for opening and closing ceremonies.

You and the girls join hands in a circle and walk toward each other from all around the circle, meeting in the middle with clasped hands raised. Say a greeting or a farewell, and walk backward into a full circle again, still holding hands.

The girls skip/walk around in a circle, saying something or singing a song.

A huddle is formed and a greeting or farewell said in different languages.

You and the girls crisscross arms, right over left, and hold hands in a friendship circle. Everyone is silent, and one person starts the friendship squeeze until it goes all the way around the circle to the person who started it.

The girls give the Girl Scout handshake to one another while they give the Girl Scout sign with their right hands.

Have a flag ceremony. Someone holds a United States flag while girls sing a patriotic song, say or listen to the pledge of allegiance, or stand in silence.

Welcoming Ceremony

An informal ceremony may be held in the very beginning of the year to welcome the girls and their families to Girl Scouting.

A formal investiture ceremony will be held a month or so later, after you have had a chance to develop with the girls the meaning of the investiture ceremony and the Girl Scout Promise and Law.

Investiture Ceremony

At an investiture ceremony, where the registered girls formally become Girl Scouts, they make the Girl Scout Promise for the first time.

This is why it is very important for you to develop the ideas of the Promise and Law with the girls before the investiture. Daisy Girl Scouts can understand them on their own level. You can explain some of the vocabulary to the girls. Then, through discussion, examples, and acting parts out, they will be able to comprehend the basics of the Girl Scout Promise and Law.

Working with the troop committee and the girls, you will be able to plan a meaningful and joyous investiture ceremony. Families should be invited, as it is the formal, symbolic beginning of Girl Scouting. If a new girl joins during the year, the troop will hold an investiture ceremony for her.

A Daisy Girl Scout wears her uniform for the first time at the investiture ceremony. The Daisy Girl Scout pin is her membership insignia and is pinned to the left side of her uniform. She wears it over her heart as all members of the movement do. Girls will also receive their Daisy Girl Scouts Beginning Certificate at the investiture.

Bridging to Brownie Girl Scouts

A bridging ceremony is held when Daisy Girl Scouts "cross the bridge" to the next age level in Girl Scouting—Brownie Girl Scouts. It is one of the important ceremonial milestones in Girl Scouting, and Daisy Girl Scouts should help as much as possible in its planning.

They will also need to learn about Brownie Girl Scouting before bridging. Girls from a sister Brownie Girl Scout troop may be invited to teach the girls the "Brownie Smile Song" and to share with them some of the facts and adventures of Brownie Girl Scouting.

The troop committee should be involved with the planning of the bridging ceremony, and families should be invited. Girls can design and produce family invitations for the event, plan refreshments, decide if they want the ceremony with the whole sister Brownie troop, just with the Brownie leader, or with a few Brownie representatives.

At the bridging ceremony, girls may receive the following insignia and recognition:

- Brownie Girl Scout pin

- World Association pin (if not already wearing it)

- one-year membership star

- Daisy Girl Scouts Ending Certificate

47

Service for Daisy Girl Scouts

Service is such an important part of Girl Scouting that it cannot be overlooked for Daisy Girl Scouts. Service is synonymous with friendship and can occur at every meeting in small ways. Larger service projects can be carried out in partnership with Brownie Girl Scout troops.

Service projects for Daisy Girl Scouts should be designed with the following suggestions in mind.

Projects should be reasonable and provide an experience that is meaningful to the girl. For example, she could go with a family member or older friend to visit someone who is shut-in and listen to and share favorite stories. Or she could help take care of a pet for someone in her family.

Projects should be of short duration. For example, the entire troop could clean up their troop meeting place one Saturday morning.

Projects should encourage learning more about Girl Scouting and bridging. For example, the girls could join with a Brownie troop to plant flowers for a neighbor or a community center.

Projects should occur as part of the ongoing troop activities. For example, service in Girl Scouting includes showing kindness during activities, sharing, and playing fairly. Girls should be encouraged to be helpful at home and at school as part of their Girl Scout experience.

Trips with Daisy Girl Scouts

Many times, troop activities are enriched by a field trip. The most important things to remember when you take your Daisy Girl Scouts on a trip are: avoid over-planning, and be conscious of safety. Also, remember that Daisy Girl Scouts tire easily and should not be pressed beyond their endurance. Always use the buddy system for troop travel.

You should have at least two adults to accompany a troop of five girls when on field trips or attending an event. Additional adults will be needed as the size of the group increases. The suggested ratio of adults to girls for field trips or events is two adults for the first five girls and one adult to each additional three girls.

With your guidance, and with parents, guardians, or other family members, your Daisy Girl Scout troop may participate in occasional overnight family camping experiences. Troop camping, in which the girls camp with only the troop leadership, is not appropriate for this age level.

Family camping can provide Daisy Girl Scouts with positive, out-of-door experiences appropriate to their age level. It will also give those girls who are bridging to Brownie Girl Scouts a better foundation for troop camping.

Measuring Troop Progress

As the Daisy Girl Scout year progresses, you will be looking at your troop as a whole and also at each girl in the troop as an individual. Observing how the troop functions and grows as a group and how each member functions and grows on her own will provide you with invaluable information and insights to help you work more effectively with the girls.

You can use the charts that follow to focus on the individual and collective development of your troop. Based on the goals stated in the program emphases, the four charts list behavior and actions that relate to each emphasis. Read over the charts at the beginning of your Daisy Girl Scout year and keep them in mind while you are working with your troop. The lists describe the ways in which you will want to see the girls grow in a manner appropriate to their age level.

From time to time during the year, look over the charts and put checks in the boxes that best indicate how the girls are doing. It will be helpful to do this with your leadership team, so you can discuss the areas where the girls' strengths lie and where they need more help.

The charts are just one means for you to measure your troop's progress. They are to be used only as a helpful personal tool and not as a basis for outside judgment of either your troop or your leadership.

Emphasis: To help each girl develop herself to achieve her full individual potential.

	Seldom	Often	Most of the time
Girls express confidence in their own abilities.	_____	_____	_____
Girls show interest in trying new things, in meeting new people.	_____	_____	_____
Girls are able to think of things to do on their own.	_____	_____	_____
Girls ask for help when they need it.	_____	_____	_____
Girls seek information, and want to know the how and why of things that affect them.	_____	_____	_____
Girls are willing to tackle and solve problems.	_____	_____	_____
Girls are interested in making things work better.			

Emphasis: To help each girl relate to others with increasing understanding, skill, and respect.

	Seldom	Often	Most of the time
Girls get along together and have a sense of troop spirit.			
Girls try to listen to each other's ideas and concerns.	___	___	___
Girls help each other, but do not take over anyone else's job.	___	___	___
Girls enjoy meeting and working with people from a variety of backgrounds.	___	___	___
Girls contribute to discussions about problems and help figure out solutions.	___	___	___
Girls help make the rules, if troop rules are needed to guide behavior and interaction.	___	___	___
Girls give support and recognition to each other's efforts, talents, and contributions.	___	___	___
Girls are able to communicate their feelings and ideas to others.	___	___	___
Girls are considerate of others.	___	___	___

Emphasis: To help each girl develop values to guide her activities and to provide the foundation for sound decision-making.

	Seldom	Often	Most of the time
Girls express ideas and beliefs freely.			
Girls choose from among a variety of activity/action possibilities.			
Girls show that they think through choices rather than just following the crowd.			
Girls try to accept their mistakes and are able to grow from them.			
Girls are open to new ways of thinking about, and doing, things.			
Girls have opportunities to test their ideas, values, and beliefs by acting on them.			
Girls are able to talk about things that are important to them.			

Emphasis: To help each girl contribute to her society through the use of her abilities and leadership skills, working in cooperation with others.

	Seldom	Often	Most of the time
Girls are able to identify what they can do to help others—in the troop, at home, and in the community.	___	___	___
Girls show interest in learning about the customs and traditions of various groups and cultures.	___	___	___
Girls show their concern about protecting their environment by doing something about it.	___	___	___
Girls decide on their own to do things for people.	___	___	___
Girls are able to see how to do a good job when they plan to help others.	___	___	___
Girls like to help and can help by doing with, rather than for, others.	___	___	___
Girls are able to think of creative and realistic ways to help where needed.	___	___	___
Girls consider each other's talents and abilities when making plans for activities.	___	___	___
Girls can organize with others for carrying out plans.	___	___	___
Girls reach out for increasing responsibility in running the troop.			

Further Ways to Measure Progress

Plan sharing meetings with the other adults who work with the children. Exchange ideas and observations about the girls and the troop. This is a good time for getting ideas about solving problems, etc.

Try keeping a brief journal of your troop meetings; it will help you remember more clearly what happened. Write what you did, how you felt, what the girls did, problems that arose, solutions to problems, things girls said, insights they had, insights you had, etc. When you go back and read it, you will discover the progress the girls are making and your own growth in working with them. You will also be able to assess areas to plan improvement and continued growth.

A notebook is helpful for keeping your Girl Scout records. Have a section on each girl, in which you place permission slips, notes from parents, and other Girl Scout records. This will save time and, when you plan meetings, you will have necessary information at your fingertips.

The Worlds of Interest

Daisy Girl Scout activities should be balanced by including activities from all five worlds of interest, active experiences (games, trips, hikes, etc.), and quiet experiences (table work, cutting, pasting, storytelling).

Activities should always allow girls experiences that encourage them to draw conclusions and learn about their world. They should be planned with the Girl Scout program emphases in mind.

The imaginations of five-year-olds are very vivid. Daisy Girl Scouts are in the process of developing language skills. Therefore, reading and storytelling are an important part of the troop meeting. At the end of each world of interest, resources are suggested for stories relating to that world. Stories can be used to prepare girls for a visit or trip, to vary activities when they are restless, or as the primary meeting activity. You might like to use your own favorite children's stories. Children also can bring in favorite books, or a family member could visit the troop and read or tell stories popular in her or his family and culture.

A resources list is included with each world of interest. These resources will aid you in developing additional activities and in understanding concepts of each world of interest. The activities described in the chapters are starting points and may be adapted to meet individual needs. All activities should reflect the interests of your troop and should be geared to the age level of Daisy Girl Scouts so the girls can complete them successfully while having fun.

The World of Well-Being

"Developing self to achieve one's full individual potential"
— Girl Scout program emphasis

Physical and emotional fitness, nutrition, health, and safety are combined in the World of Well-Being. Learning in this world can help prepare the Daisy Girl Scout for working and playing safely.

Running games are popular with this age group, as are observation activities. Daisy Girl Scouts are aware of their community and interested in learning about neighborhood helpers. Visits to firehouses, police stations, and health care facilities help girls form a concrete picture of the many individuals and services needed to keep a community operating smoothly.

Tasting and cooking activities are always fun. It is good to include familiar and unfamiliar foods in any sampling parties, but be prepared for the girls to have very strong opinions about what tastes good or bad.

Good habits begin early in life. Many health problems can be prevented by following a regimen based on the best current health knowledge in areas of exercise, rest, nutrition, and cleanliness. Daisy Girl Scouting is a good time to start lifelong good health habits.

Safety

You can play an important part in helping girls learn about personal safety. Any discussion of safety should emphasize careful behavior. Since girls need to feel at ease in asking for an adult's help, it is a good idea to enlist the aid of parents and community people as resources in any safety activities.

You can animate safety activities by using puppets or skits. Many times, role-playing a potentially unsafe situation can prepare girls to act wisely in an emergency. Be sure to adapt the role-play situations to fit the needs of the girls in your troop.

Safety Activities

Find out where fire escape routes in your meeting place are and practice using them. Practice using alternate escape routes in case the exit is blocked.

Practice making emergency phone calls on a toy phone. Girls should be able to dial the operator, report an emergency, and give their own name and address and phone number.

Talk with a fire fighter and police officer about ways girls can protect themselves in an emergency.

Learn about bicycle safety and rules of the road.

Talk about crossing streets safely. Have one girl act out the part of the crossing guard helping the others across the street. Set up traffic lights made from construction paper and "Walk" and "Don't Walk" lights. Girls should learn to recognize these even if they can't read the words. This jingle might help.

When you come to school each day,
Always walk in the safest way.
Cross at corners, watch the light,
Do the things you know are right.

Teach the girls how to answer the phone, especially when they are home alone.

61

SAFETY RULES FOR DAISY GIRL SCOUTS

Here are a few safety precautions for children. You may want to add others.

TO THE DAISY GIRL SCOUT

If a stranger tries to talk to you from a car:

Do	Don't
Tell the person you will get the leader, your parent, or another adult.	Stand too close to the car or get in the car.

When using public restrooms:

Do	Don't
Use the buddy system (take someone with you). Be sure an adult is nearby.	Play there or talk to strangers.

When using an elevator:

Do	Don't
Operate the elevator correctly. Go on the elevator with someone you know—an adult or older friend.	Play on an elevator or ride the elevator alone.

In play area:

Do	Don't
Play where you can be seen by the person taking care of you.	Play in deserted or out-of-the-way places.

Do	Don't
Play in areas that are well lighted and protected or screened by fencing.	Leave play areas without telling an adult.

Do	Don't
Be home from play before dark.	Play around construction sites, mining sites, or abandoned buildings.

Never get into a car with a stranger.
Never let anyone touch you in ways you do not like or in ways you do not think are right.
Never tell a stranger you are alone.
Never open the door to a stranger.

Time—Grooming—Health

Talk about the time children rise in the morning. What time they have to be in school . . . lunchtime . . . time Daisy Girl Scouts meet . . . bedtime.

Show the girls a calendar and how to read it. Each week, make a game of finding the meeting date on the calendar.

If the girls are interested, go over the days of the week and the months of the year. Ask each girl to tell when her birthday is, what age she is.

Girls are able to take responsibility for cleaning up the meeting place. Let one girl who knows how show the others how to sweep so they can all use the dust pan, etc.

Encourage girls to be neat and clean. Help them develop the habits of hanging up jackets or sweaters and going to the bathroom as soon as they come to the meeting place.

Girls can check to see if their hair is neat and their hands are clean before the meeting starts. A mirror is a good item to have in the room.

Girls may or may not be able to tie their shoes, put on or button their sweaters. Make a game of helping them learn. Have some garments available, with buttons to button, snap fasteners, buckles, hooks and eyes, zippers that they can practice on.

This little song is a painless way of reminding the children to brush their teeth. It is sung to the tune of "Row, Row, Row Your Boat." Have them do the up-down-circular brushing motion as they sing.

Clean, clean, clean your teeth.
Clean them every day.
Brush them, brush them, brush them, brush them,
That's the only way.

Have a nurse, dentist, doctor, or any other health professional visit the girls as a resource person. Plan active health-related activities in which all may participate.

Games for Daisy Girl Scouts

Active games are an important part of the troop. Games provide fun, learning, creativity, and adventure. They relieve tensions and encourage relaxation. They enable girls to experience the job of working in a group. They help girls learn not only to understand themselves better but also to understand others. They provide an opportunity for girls to appreciate fair play and sportsmanship.

Since girls enjoy participating in games, it is important that you be prepared to play games that are familiar to the girls, as well as to teach them new ones.

Selecting Games

Be sure the games are appropriate for the age, experience, and physical condition of the girls. Daisy Girl Scouts are able to play active games using the large muscles. Use easy games that are quickly learned. Complex games can be frustrating for girls this age. Avoid games that may encourage stereotypic thinking or offend people's beliefs or customs.

Provide opportunities for girls to participate in a variety of games: get-acquainted games, nature games, action games, international games, relays, singing games, and wide games.

Getting Ready for Games

Be interested and enthusiastic about the game yourself. Know the game well before attempting to teach it. Identify the safety hazards, anticipate the difficulties, and adapt the game to the group and situation.

Establish lines and boundaries and have available any necessary equipment.

Devise a method(s) for organizing teams that does not rely on popularity or skill.

Establish a happy atmosphere.

Check mistakes as you go along.

Encourage girls to participate and do their best.

Be patient.

Be fair in your judgments.

Show respect for each girl.

Encourage fair play and safety at all times.

Be flexible and prepared to vary or change the game.

Emphasize cooperation and playing for fun rather than winning.

Get Set, Go!

When starting the game, gather the group in a close formation so they can see and hear you well.

Give the name of the game and some interesting facts about it to help motivate interest.

Explain the game briefly, giving the basic rules, and play a short "practice" session.

Ask for questions before you start to play.

The following are games that can be played with Daisy Girl Scouts.

The Knee-Sit-Upon Circle

For years Girl Scouts have cleverly been able to rest—even when the ground was wet and there were no sit-upons in sight.

Everyone stands in a circle, touching shoulder to shoulder. Then everyone turns left, and on the count of three, each girl gently sits down on the bent knees of the person behind her. If this is done right, you should have a self-supporting, sitting circle. Enjoy the rest!

Catch the Puppy's Tail

Puppies are notorious for tail chasing. For this game you'll need a lot of open space. The girls line up, one behind the other. Each girl puts her arms around the waist of the person in front of her.

The last person in the line tucks a scarf or other piece of material into her back pocket. (If she has no pockets, she can wear a belt with the scarf tucked into it.) This last person is the puppy's tail. The person at the front of the line is the puppy's head.

The object of the game is for the puppy's head to catch its tail. The tail must try not to be caught. The fun part is that everyone's attached to one another.

At the word "Go," the head tries to catch the tail, with each girl holding on to the person in front of her. When the head catches the tail, the game is completed. The tail then becomes the head, the previous head the tail, and the game begins again. The other girls in between then take turns being the head or tail.

What Did You See?. . .or Kim's Game

This was one of Juliette Low's favorite games, and girls of all ages love it.

Put four or five things on a table. Let the girls look at the table for a minute. Then cover it.

Ask them to name one thing they saw. Increase this to two or three things as they get practice.

Another idea: When the girls are not looking, take one thing away. See if they can tell what is missing. Increase to two or three things as they get practice.

Hot and Cold

"It" goes out of the room. The group then decides on an object in the room. They choose a song or chant. As soon as they start to sing, "It" returns. As she goes near the object, the girls sing loudly. And as she goes farther away, they sing softly. This goes on until "It" guesses the object.

A Paper Statue of Myself

This is a very creative activity for Daisy Girl Scouts, who are just beginning to get a definite sense of their bodies.
You'll need:

a roll of 36-inch-wide paper	yarn
blunt-edged scissors	tape
crayons, pencils, markers	cloth scraps
glue	colored paper, wallpaper, etc.

Girls should work in pairs for this activity. After they have found someone with whom to work, the paper is spread out on the floor.

One partner lies face up on the paper, while the other traces her partner's body with a crayon, drawing around the head, neck, arms, waist, legs, all the way around the partner's body. Then they switch.

Each person will have a tracing of her body done by her partner.

Then each girl takes her paper statue and decorates it, putting in as many details as possible—eyes, nose, mouth, hair, skin, clothes, etc. She may use any of the available materials to do this.

When they're finished decorating, the girls cut out their statues along the thick crayon outlines and display. Talk about differences, similarities in decorations, size, etc.

Spot Tag

"It" runs until she tags a player. Whatever spot "It" touches—an arm, a shoulder—the player must hold, until she tags another girl.

65

Hopscotch

Countless versions of hopscotch exist—even on the same school ground. The rules are about the same, but they are played on varying diagrams, by hopping on a single foot, on both, alternately on one and then the other, and then both. If a player's marker (lagger, potsie) or she herself lands on a line, she is out. She must start again at No. 1 on her next turn.

Throw marker in space 1. Jump with right foot into 8, left foot into 7, never keeping both feet on the ground until you get "Home." Return in the same manner.

Throw marker into 1, hop on one foot, hop over 1 into 2. Hop to 3, jump and put both feet down, one in 4 and one in 5. Rest in "Heaven." Return.

Start same as picture 2. Put both feet down, one in 5 and one in 6. Hop up and land with one foot in 4 and one in 7.

Player kicks marker from square to square as she hops into it. Start at 1, hop to 11 and back to 1, then out.

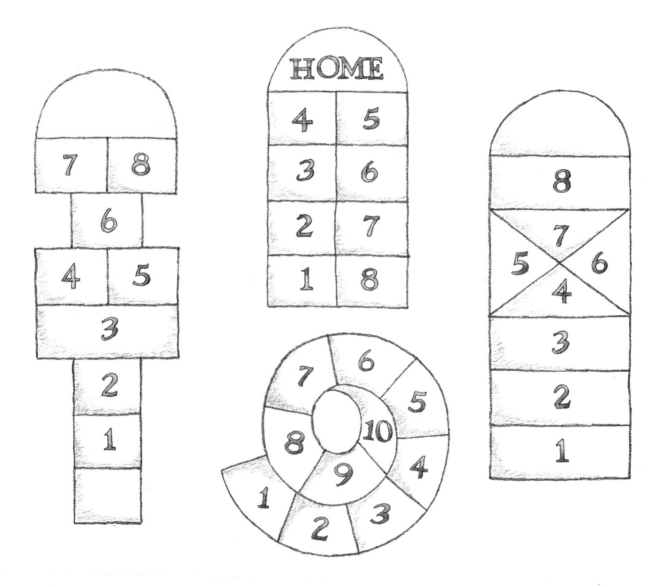

66

Daisy to Daisy

One person is the caller. The girls pair off into twos. The caller chants out different body parts that the paired players must match by touching.

Example: Caller chants "nose to nose." Partners touch nose to nose. Caller chants "head to head." Partners touch head to head, etc.

When the caller chants "Daisy to Daisy," everyone runs to find another partner, and the chants start again. Different callers can be chosen throughout the game.

This is a great way for Daisy Girl Scouts to build confidence and troop spirit.

Clues

Have a list of clues to describe something. Then give them one at a time to the girls. See how long it takes them to name what you are describing.

For example: A tree.

1. I'm tall.
2. I grow in the earth.
3. I am made of wood.
4. My top is green.
5. I have branches.
6. I have leaves.
7. Sometimes I have flowers.
8. Children climb me.
9. What am I?

More Familiar Games

Bean Bags (easier to catch than balls)	Jump Rope
	Leap Frog
Bubble Blowing	Mother, May I
Button, Button	Simon Says
Chinese Tag	Stoop Tags
Duck, Duck, Goose	Treasure Hunts
Hide and Seek	

Cooking Fun for Daisy Girl Scouts

Many girls love to cook and experiment with tastes and textures. Remember that Daisy Girl Scouts may not be able to cook without some spills and accidents. Be sure to use plastic bowls and utensils where possible. At all times use a liberal measure of patience. The following activities can help girls learn while they are having fun.

Let them practice selecting and preparing fruit—peeling bananas, sectioning oranges and grapefruits, etc.

Visit a bakery to see how breads and pastries are made.

Show them how to boil and peel a hard-boiled egg.

Let them practice arranging food on platters and serving food at home.

Making Applesauce

Use fresh apples, or other fruits available in your area and adapt the recipe. Discuss the benefits of fruit with the girls. See what they think about fruit and why it might be important.

Have little plates of applesauce, pieces of apples, and an apple, ask them what they see. See if they have any ideas about how apples are used to make applesauce.

Let the girls experience the difference between apples and applesauce. Let them look, touch, taste, smell, etc.

Raw Apple Sauce

You'll need:

paring knife	water
bowl	cups and spoons
pitcher	2 tablespoons brown sugar or honey
cutting board	
3 apples	

To make apple sauce, wash and pare apples; cut into small pieces. Grind in food grinder, in blender (with a small amount of water), or use bowl and hand masher. Add sweetening, stir, and taste.

BEYOND
If possible, plan a trip to an orchard, vineyard, or grove, where girls can pick fruit and see it on the trees, plants, and vines. Visit a mill where juice is made.

Ice Fruit Cups

You'll need:

4 cups of ripe berries, fresh or completely thawed

1½ cups honey (less if frozen berries are used)

1½ cups water

½ cup orange or lemon juice

Also:

a small paper cup for each person (and a few extras)	popsicle sticks
measuring utensils	masher
hot plate	large bowl
mixing spoons	cooking pan

After rinsing fruit, place it in bowl and let girls take turns mashing.

Place on a hot plate or stove, a pan with water and honey in it. Heat this slowly until it turns to a clear syrup, stirring occasionally. Be sure to remind girls of proper safety behavior around stoves. Everyone must be careful and attentive.

Add syrup to the fruit. Stir and mash the mixture. Add juice to fruit, continuing to stir and mash.

When it is mashed as finely as possible, spoon the mixture into the paper cups, being sure that each cup contains liquid and pulp.

Place in freezer (or let the girls take cups home to put in their own freezer if the troop does not have access to one at the meeting place). After a few minutes, when the fruit cups start to harden, place the popsicle stick into the freezing fruit pulp.

When they're frozen, the cups may be removed from the ice and they're ready to eat.

BEYOND
If there are places for collecting berries available in your area, go berry-picking. Let the girls see how the fruit grows and discover the best way to pick it. The girls may want to bring some berries home to their families.

Banana Wrap

You'll need:

bananas

orange juice or orange juice concentrate

freezer wrap

Peel banana. Coat the banana in orange juice or orange juice concentrate. Cover the banana with freezer wrap and freeze until firm.

Nutri-Bag

You'll need:

dried fruits

dry cereal

paper bag

Combine dried fruits and dry cereal in paper bag. Shake them up and serve.

Pop Fizz

You'll need:

fruit juice   a glass

club soda or seltzer   spoon

Combine half a glass of fruit juice with a half a glass of club soda or seltzer.

Veg-a-meal

You'll need:

variety of fruits and vegetables

Have girls make a vegetarian meal using fruits and vegetables.

Applewiches

You'll need:

cored apples

peanut butter

knives

Slice cored apples into rings and spread with peanut butter to make "applewiches."

Cracker Craze

You'll need:

lo-salt, lo-fat crackers   cheese

peanut butter   other healthy spreads

jelly

Let girls spread crackers with a variety of healthy spreads. Encourage girls to try different types.

Yogurt Sundaes

You'll need:

plain yogurt

cup of fruit

toppings (such as raisins, nuts, sunflower seeds, dry cereal, granola)

bowls

spoons

Have girls make their own yogurt sundaes. After placing yogurt in bowl, girls can experiment with tasting the different toppings and create their own sundaes.

Other Well-Being Activities

Each person tells "The nicest thing I could think of to do for my mother (father, brother, aunt, sister, etc.) is . . ."

Practice walking on a straight line. This helps children gain balance, dexterity, and confidence.

Practice how to pour liquids.

Have the girls bring a variety of kitchen utensils and try to guess what they are for and how they are used. Let the girls play with the utensils, and then talk about them. Put the utensils in a box or bag and see if the girls can guess, by feeling, what each thing is before they pull it out. Caution: do not place items with blades or sharp points in the bag.

Practice measuring different substances with measuring cups and spoons. Let the girls figure out which measuring devices to use for each recipe. Use standard and metric measurements.

Have girls suggest snacks they enjoy and would like to have at meetings. Help them organize a snack time. They can get food, bring it, set it up, etc. Involve parents in the snack time activity.

Practice "home tool" safety. Show the girls how to carry and use scissors, knives, garden tools, etc.

Read stories about fire safety. Visit fire stations. Have a fire official visit the troop. Act out different aspects of fire safety.

Make "family" puppets (fathers, mothers, sisters, brothers, grandmas, grandpas, aunts, uncles, cousins, etc.) by decorating old socks or paper bags. (Directions for making puppets are in the World of the Arts, pages 95 to 96.)

After children make the puppets, let them play with them. Anyone who is interested can plan a puppet show for the others. Observing the children in this process will give you a great opportunity to learn about them and their family relationships. Children often use the puppets to act out their own life experiences. Some children may reveal their concerns about family problems they are experiencing and may need special understanding.

Families come in all shapes and sizes with varying problems. Children need to believe in their own family, whatever the circumstances.

Community Helpers

Make a list of community helpers about whom the girls may be able to learn (fire fighters, doctors, nurses, safety patrolers, police, teachers, principals, mailmen or women, etc.). Help the girls arrange to have the community helpers visit the troop. Work with the adults and the girls to plan appropriate activities for the meeting. *Examples*: acting out what the person does, interviewing the person, the adult telling some interesting stories about her/his work, the adult teaching something about her/his work, etc.

Feelings

A general characteristic of Daisy Girl Scouts is being emotionally balanced, but it is still important to help them express and recognize the different ways they feel—happy, sad, angry, jealous, brave, scared, grumpy, disappointed—and the effects their feelings and moods have on themselves and others. Let them know it is all right to express their feelings. Help them see how their feelings affect their behavior. As you observe them during your experiences together, you can help them verbalize their feelings. For example: "I can see that you are disappointed. What can we do so you feel better?" or "You seem very happy today. Would you like to tell us about it?"

Have them "act out" different feelings. "Who would like to act out feeling happy, sad, angry, loving, jealous?"

After girls have played with this concept, have someone act out a feeling and others guess which one she is doing.

Girls can make up skits about feelings, draw pictures about feelings, tell stories about feelings, create music about feelings, etc.

Use hand mirrors to let girls observe their personal characteristics. Help them to discuss their images and to develop poems or songs about themselves.

Find pictures of children in different situations. Have the girls discuss what each one is probably feeling.

Help the Daisy Girl Scouts to trace the outlines of their hands and to cut them out. Explain what it means to give someone "a pat on the back," and encourage them to give the hand cut-outs to someone they feel deserves it.

As a group, come up with one thing about each girl that makes her unique or that she does well.

Use the care of pets as a way of developing values. Many girls this age will own pets and will have learned some of the responsibilities needed.

Others may have no idea of what is involved in caring for a living being. You can use situational examples such as "What would happen if someone pulled your kitten's tail?" or "What if your puppy didn't get to go for a walk?" or "What would happen if no one fed your dog?" These can stimulate other ideas for developing a caring and responsible attitude toward animals.

Lessons on poverty and hunger also can be presented at this young age. Even Daisy Girl Scouts can understand that if you don't have enough money for food, clothing, and shelter, you're living in poverty. Find out what they already know by using pictures of people in different ethnic groups, and of different backgrounds, ages, and abilities. Use these to help dispel any myths. Invite a speaker from a local human services agency to come speak. Help the girls to grow a garden to give food to others. Arrange for them to visit a nursing home to sing, to talk to, or to play games with residents. However, make sure no girl who is afraid is made to go.

The Daisy Girl Scout troop should exist in an atmosphere of trust among children and adults. Meetings should provide a place where members will be free to express, and learn to deal with, their feelings in ways beneficial to themselves and to the larger group.

Other Sources of Information

American Alliance for Health, Physical Education, and Dance
1900 Association Drive
Reston, Va. 22091

American Council on Science and Health
1995 Broadway, 18th Floor
New York, N.Y. 10023

American School Health Association
1521 S. Water Street
P.O. Box 708
Kent, Ohio 44240

Council on Health Information and Education
444 Lincoln Boulevard, No. 107
Venice, Calif. 90291

Healthy America
315 West 105th Street, #1-F
New York, N.Y. 10025

Human Development Training Institute
7574 University Avenue
La Mesa, Calif. 92041

National Mental Health Association
1021 Prince Street
Alexandria, Va. 22314

National Wellness Institute
South Hall
University of Wisconsin — Stevens Point
    Foundation
Stevens Point, Wis. 54481

Nutrition Education Association
P.O. Box 20301
3647 Glen Haven
Houston, Texas 77225

Office of Disease Prevention and Health Promotion
National Health Information Center
P.O. Box 1133
Washington, D.C. 20013

Society for Nutrition Education
1700 Broadway, Suite 300
Oakland, Calif. 94612

Wellness Associates
Box 5433-E
Mill Valley, Calif. 94942

The World of People

"Relating to others with increasing understanding, skill, and respect"
— Girl Scout program emphasis

Through activities in the World of People, Daisy Girl Scouts explore many of the cultures in our world family. This knowledge will help form a foundation of respect for diversities and similarities and for the contributions of a variety of people and cultures. By the time girls reach the age to enter their first troop, they will be aware of many differences and similarities among people. They may have already formed opinions and may display feelings about cultures and people. Some children may need gentle encouragement to be accepting of girls and adults from diverse groups. Your role is to encourage the respect for diversity that is such an important part of Girl Scouting.

In any activity, you will want to encourage girls to:

• be open-minded

• notice the qualities people have in common, while remembering differences

• understand that, while many values are universal, different racial, religious, and cultural groups value different things

Any World of People activity should begin with a very short discussion of the experiences girls have had relating to that activity.

Example: When beginning a holiday celebration, focus on ways holidays are celebrated in each girl's family. Encourage the girls to share unique aspects of their culture with the group. Also, parents and family members can be valuable resources in any discussion of heritage or traditions.

One of the goals of Girl Scouting is to help every girl feel she is unique and understand that everyone is different and therefore special. World of People activities, and the sensitive caring way in which they are presented, will enhance the Daisy Girl Scout's self-esteem.

Celebrations

". . . to be a sister to every Girl Scout . . ."
—Girl Scout Law

Holidays, feast days, religious celebrations—and the ways they are celebrated—differ according to culture, tradition, and background. These special days are rooted in a history that sometimes goes back many centuries. Some days are well known, and others are celebrated only by small groups in a larger cultural group or regional section. The United States, as a country of diverse populations, has incorporated many holidays and religious celebrations into its traditional calendar. These reflect some of the customs of the many peoples who make up this country.

It is especially important to be receptive to the diversity of holidays that may be celebrated by the girls in the troop. One way to do this is to consult the parents and/or family members of girls when planning any holiday activity. The families can describe celebrations that have meaning for them. With planning and assistance from families and community resources, learning about special days can be an excellent opportunity for cultural sharing.

Birthdays

> " . . . to be cheerful . . . "
>
> —Girl Scout Law

Daisy Girl Scouts love birthday celebrations! Be sure to observe the birthdays of the girls in the troop. Encourage girls to talk about the ways birthdays are celebrated in their families. Families have many ways of expressing celebrations. Some let birthday children have a meal of their own choice; others say the child with the birthday invites and serves others.

In Greece, the day of the saint the person is named after is celebrated rather than the birthday. The day starts with a church service. Friends and relatives visit during the day and bring a small gift. A special meal is served, ending with feta cheese and fresh fruit. Cookies are eaten instead of cake.

Special Days

> " . . . to show respect for myself and others through my words and actions . . . "
>
> —Girl Scout Law

"Special days" can be used to illustrate the customs of many cultures. Since celebration usually shows only one aspect of a particular culture, it can be supplemented with information about the life-styles, food, values, and beliefs of that culture. Consultants, or information obtained from the public library, can be used to round out any exploration.

There are many traditional American holidays to consider: Thanksgiving, New Year, Halloween, birthdays of various presidents, Labor Day, Memorial Day, celebrations of national heros and heroines, etc. In addition to these, there are the celebrations of other countries.

Mexico

Mexican Independence Day, September 16, is celebrated in memory of the day in 1810 when a priest called Hidalgo issued a call to the people of Mexico to revolt against Spain.

Fiesta!

Hold a fiesta or party. Serve Mexican hot chocolate and pan dulce (sweet bread). Play a recording of a Mexican mariachi band. Break a piñata filled with candy.

Piñata

A piñata is sometimes a clay jar covered with colored crepe paper in a shape of an animal, bird, or flower. Many piñatas are made out of papier-mâché.

Piñatas are filled with candies, popcorn, pennies, or small party favors. They are hung from the ceiling or a tree branch by rope. Children take turns trying to break the piñata while blindfolded. Each child, in turn, is given a stick and allowed three strokes with the stick to break the piñata. When someone breaks it and the contents are scattered, everyone scrambles for them!

Papier-Mâché Piñata

1. Blow up a balloon and attach it to a string.

2. Cover with five layers of papier-mâché (torn strips of newspaper dipped in liquid starch or flour and water paste). Dry thoroughly between layers.

3. When final layer is dry, pop balloon and pull through opening.

4. Paint the piñata and fill with candy.

For another special occasion, you might make cinnamon crisps, a favorite dessert of the children of

Mexico. All you need are some flour, tortillas, butter, cinnamon, and sugar. Spread the tortillas with butter. Mix the cinnamon and sugar together. Sprinkle the cinnamon sugar mixture on the tortillas. Put them under the broiler until toasted.

Japan

The sichi-go-san birthday festival is celebrated on November 15. On this day, the children of Japan who are 7 (shichi), 5 (go), and 3 (san) dress in their best clothes and visit shrines with their parents. Sweets and paper good luck talismans are sometimes purchased at the shrines.

Good Luck Talismans

Make good luck talismans (charms) out of red paper. Cut thin rectangular strips of bright (origami or tissue) paper. Decorate the strips with gummed gold circles or seals and attach a string at the top. Fringe the bottom if desired.

Netherlands

Sinterklass, December 6. In the Netherlands, girls and boys celebrate the birthday of St. Nicholas, the children's saint, on this day. Candy and gifts with funny poems enclosed are given to children.

Sinterklass Stars

To make Sinterklass stars, use a pattern and cut stars from lightweight cardboard (Botany paper is good). Color the stars red and blue, and tie three stars together on different lengths of cord or yarn.

Israel

Have you ever heard of a birthday for trees? In Israel, Tu bi-Shevat is a holiday to honor trees. It is celebrated in the spring. Jewish people in other parts of the world may also celebrate Tu bi-Shevat, but in Israel, the whole country celebrates. Tu bi-Shevat (TOO bish VAT) means the fifteenth day of the Hebrew month of Shevat and is also referred to as the New Year for Trees.

In ancient times, the Jewish people of Israel planted a tree for every child born during the year. A cypress tree was planted for every girl and a cedar tree for every boy. Today, the children of Israel plant trees on Tu bi-Shevat and talk about the many things that trees give them. On this festival day, they eat the almonds, figs, oranges, and other fruit that grow on the trees of Israel.

In most parts of the United States and Canada and in many other countries, citizens also have days or weeks for planting trees. In the United States we call the celebration Arbor Day. Some states offer prizes to organizations and people who plant the most trees. You can find out if your state celebrates Arbor Day, or you can celebrate it in the same way that the children of Israel celebrate Tu bi-Shevat.

Vietnam

Tet Trung-Thu (mid-autumn festival), one of the favorite holidays for Vietnamese children, is celebrated in September or October on the day of the full moon. Families make "moon" cakes of rice, filled with sugar, peanuts, raisins, and other treats. Then children parade through the streets with paper lanterns, celebrating the moon and the autumn.

Lanterns and Moon Cakes

Girls can make paper lanterns that will fit over flashlights and parade around the room shining their flashlight lanterns.

Invent a recipe for moon cakes, using cooked rice, eggs, peanuts, raisins, figs, coconut, etc. Organize a cooking activity to make moon cakes. Play some Vietnamese folk songs or instrumental records.

Peru

During the carnival at Arequipa, in the middle of February (summertime for Peruvians), there are costume parades, dancing in the streets, and cascaron-throwing. Cascarones are eggs that have been emptied, refilled with confetti or colored water, and sealed.

Boys and girls make lots of these, filling some with confetti and others with colored water. Then they go out into the hot Peruvian summer sun, and as part of the carnival, everyone (adults and children) has a huge water throw. They throw the water eggs and the confetti eggs. Bags and buckets of water are splashed. It's a colorful way to cool off because, once the people are wet, the colored confetti sticks to them. Then everyone looks like a walking rainbow.

Cascarones

On a very hot day, girls could make cascarones or fill different-colored balloons with uncolored water and have a cascaron or water-balloon catch. They can throw the cascarones/balloons back and forth, catching them and stepping further and further apart until the cascaron/balloon breaks.

To empty an egg, put two pinholes in each end of the egg. Make the hole at the wide end of the egg bigger than the other. Blow through the little hole. The egg should come out the larger hole. Save the eggs and make a feast of scrambled eggs.

To fill the egg, seal the small hole with glue and make the large hole big enough to pour in water or drop in little pieces of confetti.

To close the egg, you can use plastic wrap glued over the opening or inside of the opening of the egg.

India

Onam is celebrated in Kerala in South India, a warm, moist, lush land. Harvests are plentiful and include coconuts, tapioca plants, yellow-green rice, tea, and pepper.

The seasonal heavy rains help to make the land productive. When the strongest rains are over, the people of Kerala have a great festival called Onam. The festival also celebrates a legendary king named Mahabali. His mythical reign was one of peace, equality, and happiness for Kerala.

At Onam, people say the king's spirit visits them, and everyone wants him to feel that his people are happy and still living peaceful, healthy, prosperous lives. Everything is cleaned. Floors are decorated with colored chalk designs, and at dawn children collect flowers from which women weave flower carpets. Then everyone goes from home to home to look at the beautiful, fragrant carpets before they begin to wither.

The father or grandfather in each family gives gifts of sunny-yellow clothing to all the children. The color of the cloth is the symbol of harvest.

People worship and give thanks. Young girls do special festival dances. Some people who live near the sea have boat races while others cheer. There is a great deal of singing, dancing, feasting, and laughing.

Some of the traditional foods that are cooked at Onam are boiled bananas/plantains, battered and fried vegetables, fried round flat bread (pappadam), sweet pickles, curried vegetables with peppers, puddings, and sweets dipped in honey.

Onam

After the girls have learned about the holiday, you can re-create your own Onam in your troop meeting place. Flower carpets can be woven out of large, bright strips of paper. Everything can be cleaned. Floors can be decorated with large pieces of mural paper designed with colored chalk. Girls can "visit" to see each other's rugs. Headbands the color of the sun can be made and given to the girls. Recorded Indian music can be played, and a cooking session can be planned to make some of the traditional Onam foods to eat. If anyone knows any of the traditional Onam dances, that person can be invited to teach or share the dance with the troop.

China

Yuan Tan (Chinese New Year). The date of this holiday in the United States falls on the second new moon after the winter solstice (usually within the last two weeks of January and first two weeks of February). It is everyone's birthday.

Everything is cleaned. New clothes and new shoes are worn (it's bad luck to wear old shoes in the New Year). Windows and doors are sealed and decorated with pieces of red paper as symbols of good luck and happiness. Old debts are paid off.

On New Year's Eve, a special dinner is eaten leisurely and quietly. At midnight, members of the family formally and ceremoniously greet one another. In order by age, from a sitting position, the family members bow to the elders. One at a time, they touch the ground with their foreheads (K'o T'ou, or in English "Kowtow") and wish the elders a happy New Year. The children are given little red envelopes containing inscribed coins on which is printed "New Happiness for the New Year!" in silver or gold.

On the first day of the New Year, after the seals on the doors and windows have been broken, everyone must be very polite and especially considerate. Most people stay home with their families on New Year's Day and have a very quiet, well-behaved day to worship and remember their ancestors.

However, for fourteen days after New Year's Day there are parties, singing, dancing, feasts, exchanges of greeting cards, food, and good wishes.

The holiday ends with a parade of lanterns led by a huge paper dragon, the Chinese symbol of strength and goodness.

Happy New Year!

Re-create your own Chinese New Year with your troop, acting it out, making props, etc. Make egg drop soup.

6 cups chicken broth

¼ teaspoon salt

4 eggs (beaten)

Heat broth to boiling. Add beaten eggs and salt. While stirring, bring to a boil again. Serve.

American Indian

On the fourth Friday of September, many states in the United States honor the American Indian people in this country. The holiday is called American Indian Day.

American Indian Day

Learn about the tribes of your area and their customs. How did they live, and what happened to them?

Use libraries, historians, and other community resources to learn about the traditional cooking, dances, clothing, holidays, values, and life-styles of your local tribes.

Plan activities with the girls to celebrate American Indian Day. Cook and eat a traditional dish, make a copy of a ceremonial costume, invite someone to demonstrate a dance, listen to the music of different tribes, or reenact a ceremony after learning about it.

Scandinavia

Leif Ericson Day, October 9, celebrates the Norse explorer who, it is believed, was one of the first European people to discover what is now Iceland, Greenland, and parts of North America.

In Viking Days

A story about Leif Ericson could be read to the girls. They could draw pictures about the story, act parts of it out, or make up their own stories about discovering things. They could also learn about Viking life, make models of Viking ships, see a film about the Vikings, etc.

Africa

Kwanza, meaning "fresh fruits," is the name of a holiday that commemorates African harvest festivals. It is now celebrated by families in countries all over the world. The holiday begins on December 25 and lasts for a week. It celebrates the family and its togetherness. People have daily parties, giving homegrown and homemade gifts to each other. They light candles (mishumaas) and drink from a family cup (kibombe) at a big feast on New Year's Day.

Mishumaas and Kibombe

Have your own one-day Kwanza celebration with your troop and their families after the troop has learned about the holiday. Families can make homemade dishes and bring them to share with each other. Mishumaas may be lit, and people may drink symbolically from the kibombe by pouring the beverage into individual cups from the kibombe to celebrate the togetherness and unity of the troop and their families.

Canada

Nova Scotia Apple Blossom Day is in late May or early June. When all the apple blossoms are in bloom, people have parades, dances, and barbecues.

Apple Blossoms and Barbecues

The girls in your troop can learn about apple trees and blossoms and plan their own parade, dance, and barbecue.

Australia

Australia Day, January 26, marks the founding of Australia in 1788. It is an Australian national holiday.

Kookaburra

Learn the song "Kookaburra" and sing it at the meeting. Have each girl draw a picture of what she thinks a kookaburra looks like. Then look through a book to try and find pictures of other animals native to Australia (koala, kangaroo, duck-billed platypus). *Note:* A kookaburra is a large brown bird with a light breast.

Moomba Festival

The Moomba Festival is a celebration that lasts eleven days! "Moomba" is an Aborigine word that means "get together to have fun." The Aborigines are the Native Australians in Australia.

At the Moomba Festival, there are usually water shows, boat races, other sports activities, theatre and music presentations. There are always lots of clowns in the Moomba parade. Girls can make up their faces in clown make-up, plan sporting events or contests, music and theatre activities and have their own Moomba Festival!

Germany

First Day of School

To celebrate the first day of school, some Germans give a special treat to their children. They make large 3-foot paper cones and fill them with goodies and give them to their offspring on the first day of school. Sometimes kids make them for each other and exchange them as presents!

You'll need:

oak tag or flexible cardboard

tissue or crepe paper to line the cone

ribbon

glue

tape

colored paper or scraps of wrapping paper to decorate the outside of the cone

1. First you cut a curved cone shape out of the oak tag or cardboard. (See illustration.)

2. Then roll the cardboard into a cone shape until the edges overlap one another by a few inches. Tape the edges closed.

3. Line the entire inside of the cone with a sheet of crepe paper so that the crepe paper sticks up out of the cone all the way around the top about 6 inches.

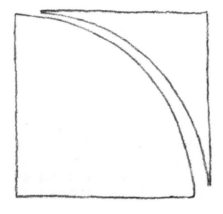

France

Mardi Gras

"Mardi Gras" means "Fat Tuesday" in French. Many countries celebrate Mardi Gras. Every year in New Orleans, Louisiana, there is a big Mardi Gras festival. It's a time when people feast, dance, have fun, wear costumes, have a parade, throw confetti, etc., before the long time of fasting or "giving something up" for the Lenten season.

A common treat that children enjoy during Mardi Gras is raspberry lemonade and pancakes. Girls can plan a Mardi Gras parade and have raspberry lemonade and pancakes for a snack.

Raspberry Lemonade

For ten people, you'll need:

12 ounces of lemonade concentrate (frozen)

10 ounces of frozen raspberries

8 cups of water

Mix ingredients in a blender and serve.

Pancake Snack

For ten people, you'll need:

8 eggs

8 cups of flour

1 cup of safflower or corn oil

1 teaspoon of baking soda

1 teaspoon of salt

Beat eggs and oil together. Add the flour, baking soda and salt to the mixture. Cook pancakes. Serve them hot with honey, syrup, yogurt, or jam.

4. Glue the crepe paper to the inside of the cone so it doesn't fall out.

5. Decorate the cone with the colored paper and/or wrapping paper scraps.

6. Fill the cone with goodies.

7. Tie the crepe paper at the top of the cone closed with the ribbon.

Hawaii

Kamehameha Day

Every year in June, people in Hawaii celebrate one of their great leaders who lived when Hawaii had kings (over two hundred years ago). His name was Kamehameha I. There is a parade, a feast, flowers, and singing.

Girls can celebrate by making symbolic leis (flower wreaths) out of paper, having a feast, and talking about leadership.

International Games

"...to be honest, to be fair...to be friendly and considerate..."
—Girl Scout Law

Languages, customs, and cultures may differ, but one fact remains true everywhere on the globe—children enjoy playing games. International games provide a pleasant way to introduce international friendship to Daisy Girl Scouts. The following games are adapted from *World Games and Recipes*, published by the World Association of Girl Guides and Girl Scouts. They are listed by country of origin.

Zambia

Crocodile, May I Cross the River?

This game can be played indoors or out. A line is marked on the ground, and the "crocodile" stands on one side of it facing the girls. The girls come to the river bank (the line) chanting, "Crocodile, crocodile, may I cross your river?" The crocodile answers "No!"

This is repeated until the crocodile says "Yes, if you give me a yellow flower" (or a safety pin, a stone, anything else that is easily available).

The first girl to find whatever is asked for and bring it to the river bank is allowed to cross the river.

The game continues until all the girls are across.

Argentina

El Gato y el Raton ("Cat and Mouse")

Players join hands in a circle. One player, Mouse, stands inside the circle. Another, Cat, stands outside the circle, facing Mouse.

CAT: Mouse, what are you doing in my vineyard?

MOUSE: Eating grapes.
(Cat holds her hand out toward Mouse.)

CAT: Give me some.
(Mouse reaches through the circle and pretends to put some grapes into Cat's hands.)

MOUSE: Here they are.

CAT: Give me more.
(This may be repeated as often as Mouse wishes to answer: "Here they are.") Then,

CAT: Give me more.

MOUSE: No!

CAT: I'll catch you.

MOUSE: If you can.

Mouse runs and Cat chases her. The players in the circle try to protect Mouse. If Cat enters the circle by going under joined hands, they let Mouse out. If both Cat and Mouse are outside the circle, they help Mouse enter. When Cat catches Mouse, two other players take their places and play begins again.

Sudan

The Leopard Trap

Two players make a "bridge" or "trap" with their raised arms in the middle of the room. The other players form a large circle and dance around, passing through the trap. The circling players sing a song and clap to its rhythm.

In Sudan, the girls chant: "Lion and leopard, lion and leopard, two night hunters, lion and leopard, lion and leopard, hunt their prey."

On the last syllable, the trap falls. A player is caught and must drop out. The others continue circling and singing until another player is caught.

The two captured players form another trap.

The game goes on in the same way until only two players remain untrapped. These are the winners.

Nigeria

Shadow Baby

The group picks someone to be the "guesser." The guesser leaves the room. Then the group picks someone to be the "shadow baby." The shadow baby lies on the ground or the floor while the group outlines her body shape with shells, pebbles, chalk, or sticks. The "baby" then stands up and rejoins the group. Her shadow outline is on the ground. Someone gets the guesser to come back to the group. The guesser then has to guess who is the "shadow baby" by looking at the outline and looking at the people in the group.

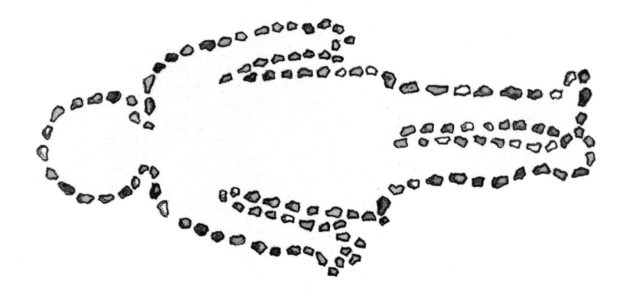

Brazil

Hit the Stone Off the Stick

Hammer a stick (1–2 feet long) into the ground. Draw a circle 6 inches in diameter around the stick. Put a flat, small stone on top of the stick. Girls stand in a circle 4 feet away from the stick and try to knock the stone off the stick by throwing another small stone at it. If a girl knocks off the stone outside the little 6-inch circle, she scores one point. If the stone falls inside the 6-inch circle, or if she misses hitting the stone, she scores 0. First person to get '7' wins.

Additional World of People Activities

Make a people album, using snapshots or drawings.

Create hats and caps from different parts of the world using paper plates and fabric scraps. Talk about the ways clothing is changed according to climate and natural resources.

Visit a store, look for items that are important, and record the country of origin on a world map.

Other Sources of Information

The Bilingual Publications Company
1966 Broadway
New York, N.Y. 10023

Council of Interracial Books for Children, Inc.
1841 Broadway
New York, N.Y. 10023

Green Circle Program, Inc.
1300 Spruce Street
Philadelphia, Pa. 19107

Information Center on Children's Cultures
331 East 38th Street
New York, N.Y. 10016

Japanese American Curriculum Project
414 East Third Avenue
P.O. Box 367
San Mateo, Calif. 94401

National Clearinghouse for Bilingual Education
1300 Wilson Boulevard, Suite B2-11
Rosslyn, Va. 22209

New York Public Library
Office of Children's Services
455 Fifth Avenue
New York, N.Y. 10036

U.S. Board on Books for Young People
c/o International Reading Association
800 Barksdale Road
Newark, Del. 19714

The World of Today and Tomorrow

Why? What? How? When? Maybe if. . . . Look at this!

Children love to learn about what makes things work and why and how they work. They are capable of being good observers and experimenters. Some may show the patience and interest of a Pasteur, trying things over and over again as if to prove that what they see is real. Their world is one of constant discovery as they try out new things for themselves.

As a leader, you will be able to provide the girls with opportunities for discovery while letting them seek the answers for themselves. Making discoveries and learning about themselves and their world is exciting for Daisy Girl Scouts as they experience the World of Today and Tomorrow.

Some Today and Tomorrow Activities

Things with Numbers

Have girls think of as many things as they can that have numbers on or in them. Make a list. Then help them bring in as many things on the list as possible to observe, play with, talk about, figure out, and study.

Some possibilities: rulers, calendars, scales, stopwatches, measuring tapes, spoons, cups, thermometers, telephones, clocks, typewriters, radios, telephone books, etc.

Seesaw Balance

You'll need:

blocks or bricks

a round block

wedge-shaped blocks

long planks or pieces of wood

different things to balance

See if girls can figure out how to make a seesaw balance using a plank, a round block (for underneath pivot), and two blocks for wedges.

After they make the balance, let them experiment with different objects, trying to see which things are heavier, lighter, equal, etc.

Food and Heat

You'll need:

different types of food to heat (apples, peaches, bread, popcorn, eggs, butter, etc.)

hot plate

big pan with lid

water or fat

Have the girls look at the raw foods and try to imagine what will happen to each one as it is heated.

Let them be involved in finding out what happens to each one. Eat up the results of the experiment!

Changing Sugar

You'll need:

sugar cubes	hot plate
water	wooden spoon
pans	bowls

Girls can see physical and chemical changes when they try dissolving, retaining through evaporating, and burning sugar. Dissolving sugar and retaining it through evaporation produce physical changes. When sugar is burned, it goes through a chemical change. After the two physical changes have taken place, the taste and general characteristics of sugar remain essentially the same. But all the characteristics of sugar are altered during the chemical change of burning.

The girls crumble the sugar. Then they place some sugar in water to be dissolved. At each step, they should taste to see if the taste is still sweet.

The water is heated and boiled off until about 8 ounces of the solution remain in the pan. Pour half of this into a bowl and let it sit for several days. The remaining water should evaporate, and sugar should be left in the bowl. Let the girls discover the results for themselves without telling them yourself.

Heat the remaining solution in the pan until it burns. The girls will notice the changes in smell, color, and texture. And when it has cooled off and been scraped to sample, they will notice the taste has changed.

Classifying Game

A "set" is a group of things that are similar in some way.

Have the girls make sets on their own, by observing and grouping objects that are similar in some way. Example: a set of rocks, a set of green pencils, a set of toes, a set of Girl Scouts, a set of red socks, a set of black shoes, etc.

To play the game:

One person is the caller, the others are the players.

As the leader teaching them the game, you should be the caller first. After the girls understand the game, they can take turns being the caller.

The caller calls out different set names and the girls who are members of that set follow the caller's directions. Example:

"All girls wearing brown shoes, stand together."
"All girls who like pizza, raise their hands."
"All girls with brown eyes, clap their hands."

Girls who fit any of the caller's set names do what the caller directs (stand together, raise hands, clap hands, etc.)

Crystals

When combined, the following chemicals react with salt to form crystals. You'll need, per girl or pair of girls:

4 tablespoons nonoxidized table salt	aluminum pie tin
4 tablespoons liquid bluing	porous materials—sponge, cork, bark, moss, driftwood
4 tablespoons water	food coloring as desired
1 tablespoon ammonia	

Arrange the porous materials in the pie tin.

Mix the salt, bluing, water, and ammonia together in a bowl or measuring cup.

Spoon the mixture over the objects in the tin until the solution covers the bottom of the tin.

For color, drop a small amount of food coloring into the solution in the tin. Put the tin in a safe place for 4 to 5 days without moving it. Watch it change!

A *Magnifying Glass*

You'll need:

different types of magnifying glasses—stands, hand glasses, etc.

different objects—leaves, crayons, pencils, paper, shells, rocks, feathers, cloth, letters written on paper, flowers, grains of sugar and salt.

Let the girls play/work with the materials to see what they can discover about magnifying glasses. Have a sharing time in which they discuss what they have found. Girls may want to look at their hands, toes, hair, fingernails, at each other's faces, etc., under the glass.

My *Finger Is Unique!*

Have girls use stamp pads and paper to compare fingerprints. See if they notice that each one is different.

Troop Height and Weight

You'll need:

chart paper

crayons

measuring sticks (yard or meter)

scale

In the beginning of the troop meeting year, have the girls measure each other in height and weight.

As time passes, they may measure themselves and chart the new measurements to see how they are changing.

Experiment with Water

Half fill a jar with water. Put something in the water. Some things float and some things sink. Some dissolve and other things absorb well. Try some of these: cocoa, soap, liquid detergent, oil, flour, sand, soil, oatmeal, prunes, a paper towel. Let the jar and the things you put in the water sit for a while and see what happens. Then stir it and see if there is any difference.

There's Air in My Soda!

To help girls observe some characteristics about air, carbon dioxide, soda, and soda bubbles, you'll need:

small bottles of carbon-ated soda

balloons

vinegar

baking soda

empty bottles

cups

funnel

Pour some soda in a cup. Let the girls look at and taste the soda and feel, see, and hear the soda bubbles when they put their faces above the soda cup.

Have girls place a balloon over the neck of the carbonated soda in the bottle. Let them see what happens, and talk with them about what they think is happening. The carbon dioxide gas in the soda is escaping through the bottle neck and into the balloon, blowing the balloon up.

Next, girls can make their own carbon dioxide solution by mixing vinegar and baking soda. They can funnel the solution into an empty bottle and see if a balloon put on top of the bottle expands.

Seeds

Collect different types of seeds, categorize them, and then sprout them to see how they grow.

One of the best sprouting containers is a large-mouthed fruit jar prepared as follows:

1. Cut a piece of new clean screen wire to fit over the mouth of the jar.

2. Hold the screen wire in place with an ordinary canning ring-lid holder.

3. Sprouts in this container may easily be flushed and drained.

Use mung beans or soybeans for sprouting. Beans can be sprouted in almost any container that has some sort of holes to allow for drainage. The beans will swell to over six times their original size, so allow plenty of room.

To sprout beans:

1. Soak the beans overnight.

2. Remove from water. Drain. Place in the sprouting container and place it on its side in a warm, dark spot.

3. Pour lukewarm water over the beans at least five or six times a day, making sure you flush them thoroughly. Drain well.

4. In three to six days, the beans will have grown sprouts.

These bean sprouts are good to eat as is. Or they may be added to salads or used in sandwiches.

Candle-Making

Melting wax and creating things is an example of physical change.

You'll need:

wax	oil
old candles	containers to serve as molds for the wax (milk cartons, tin cans, glass, aluminum containers, etc.)
crayons	
string for wicks	
coffee can	
water	metal washers
hot plate	pencils

Place wax in coffee can. Place can in pan of water on hot plate. Melt the wax this way using low heat.

Add crayons for color. This may make smoky, smelly candles. Grease the mold with vegetable oil. Fill the mold with melted wax.

Tie a washer to the wick (the wick should be about 4 inches longer than the candle). Let the wick drop down into the center of the mold. Put a pencil across the top of the mold, wrap the other end of the wick around it.

Let candle sit and cool completely. Remove candle from mold.

Experiment with Sound

How does sound travel? How can you hear sound better?

You will need:

a table or counter top

two metal spoons

an aquarium or gallon jug filled with water

string

paper cups

Girls will listen to the tapping of spoons and hear how sound moves differently through different materials.

Hold the spoons about three feet away from the girls and ask them to listen as two spoons are tapped together. Ask what the sound traveled through to get there. Have the girls rest their ears on one end of the table while someone taps a spoon at the other end. Ask again what the sound traveled through. Now have the girls rest one ear on the side of an aquarium or one at a time against the side of a jug. Put two spoons into the water and tap them together. Have girls listen for differences in the sound. Again ask what the sound traveled through. Now take a piece of string three feet in length and tie a spoon in the middle. Have a girl wrap each end of the string to each of her index fingers. Ask her to place her fingers in her ears and bend forward slightly so that the spoon dangles freely. Tap the spoon with another spoon. Guide the group in concluding that sound travels better through solids and liquids than through air.

Sounds We Make

Girls can experiment with sounds they can make.

You'll need:

tubes

megaphone

tape recorder

paper cups

Have the girls touch their throats while humming, coughing, laughing, talking, or shouting. Let them experiment with talking through a tube, megaphone, tape recorder. Let them see how they can magnify sound. Have them cup their hands behind their ears. Then cut out the bottoms of paper cups and place them over their ears. Have them listen to different things with their cups. You might ask them about animals that have larger ears and what this might mean.

Environmental Sounds

Have girls record sounds from the environment.

You'll need:

tape recorder

tape

Take girls on a walk out-of-doors. Help them record sounds they hear. When they return to the meeting place, play the tape back to them and have them try to remember what the sounds were.

Discovery Boxes

Ordinary shoe boxes can become treasure chests of science discovery activities. Put related items in a box. Girls can handle the materials in each box on their own or with a partner. Here are some ideas of items to put in boxes. Be prepared to ask girls some directive questions. Girls can help assemble these boxes, too.

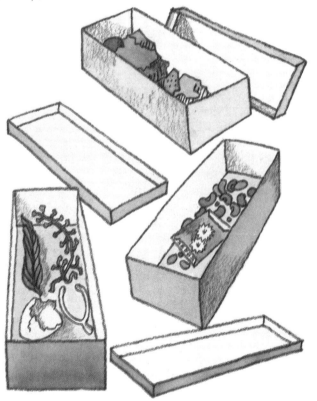

SEEDS
Look for a variety of seeds. You might include pictures of the plant and see if girls can guess which seeds go with which plants. Ask them about different ways seeds may be used. Include some seeds that are not cultivated.

ROCKS
Try and find a range of color, size, and shape. If possible, provide a magnifying glass. Girls can rub rocks on blank paper to see if they leave colored marks. Encourage girls to add to the collection.

TOOLS AND MACHINES
Make a collection of simple hand tools or machinery that girls can examine. Ask them to explain what each thing does.

A PIECE OF THE WHOLE
Assemble a collection of fragments from familiar items, for example, egg shell, a chicken bone, a pine needle, grape stems, feather, hair strand. Girls can guess what they have pieces of.

SENSE BOXES
Assemble boxes for each sense, for example, items that have an aroma or smell or items that can be identified by touch. Include a blindfold so that girls may use only one sense in identifying what they have. If testing taste, be sure to observe good sanitation and storage.

Make a Periscope

Here is a shoe box activity that each girl can make for herself.

You will need:

a shoe box	masking tape
2 small mirrors	paint
glue	scissors

Cut two windows from the long side of the box as illustrated. Glue or tape mirrors across from each window. To do this, put in the top mirror, then put in the bottom one, adjusting it until it catches the reflection of the top one and you can see out the top. Glue the bottom mirror in place. Put the lid on the box and seal it with the tape.

Experiment with Snow

You'll need:

snow

3 bowls

Divide snow into three small bowls. Put one in the freezer, one in the refrigerator, and one on a table. Check them in thirty minutes. What has happened to each?

Math Shapes

Girls can learn the names of some basic math shapes: circle, square, triangle, rectangle, and ellipse or oval. To help reinforce their learning, you can ask the girls to draw pictures using the shapes. Another method is to have them find examples of the shape in real life.

Counting Games and Songs

Many games and songs can be used to reinforce beginning arithmetic skills. One simple game can be a number scavenger hunt. Girls must find something that has parts in the amount that they are looking for. Numbers can be in sequence or not. For example, the numbers in the scavenger hunt might be 5, 1, 10, etc. A glove has five fingers and could be used as the find for number five, and so on.

Today and Tomorrow in the Community

". . .To help where I am needed. . ."
—Girl Scout Law

Tidy up the ground around the meeting place, the school yard, the streets where the girls live. Put papers in trash cans. Help a sister troop with a flower planting project. Water plants for family and neighbors.

Safety Tours

Look around the neighborhood to see how many things there are that keep people safe—traffic lights, stop signs, crosswalks, fire hydrants, street lights, play areas, bicycle paths.

Public Service

Find out about the people who make the town or city a safe place—policemen, firemen, street cleaners, street repair crews, trash collectors, crossing guards, etc. Invite someone to a meeting to share the ways he or she makes the city safe, or show a short film from a library.

Field Trips

Arrange for a trip to a city hall, library, gas and light company, airport, train station, a special garden, a park, a nearby stable, a farmyard. Talk about what the girls may expect to see. Have the girls tell what they liked best. Ask them to draw a picture of something they remembered.

U.S. Mail

Help the girls learn how a letter or postcard gets from one place to another. Visit a post office. If possible, arrange for a behind-the-scenes tour. Talk about postage stamps. Encourage girls to collect stamps from the mail received at home. Help them send a letter to themselves to find out firsthand how the mail works.

The Work People Do

Find out some of the things people do in the world of work. Ask the girls if they know what their parents do at work—or perhaps what some relative, friend, or neighbor does.

Ask them if they know how people doing different kinds of work might be very important to them: the carpenter, the dentist, the newspaper reporter, a computer programmer, a sculptor, a dancer, etc.

Invite to a meeting or visit someone who might have an interesting job and who could provide an inside look or direct experience.

Other Sources of Information

American National Red Cross
Seventeenth and D Streets, N.W.
Washington, D.C. 20006

Consumer Information Center
General Services Administration
Washington, D.C. 20405

Environmental Protection Agency
401 M Street, S.W.
Washington, D.C. 20460

ERIC Clearinghouse for Science, Math and
        Environmental Education
Ohio State University
1200 Chambers Road, Room 310
Columbus, Ohio 43212

ERIC Clearinghouse for Social Studies/Social
        Science Education
Indiana University
Social Studies Development Center
2805 East 10th Street
Bloomington, Ind. 47405

National Institute of Science
Graduate Office
Prairie View A & M University
Prairie View, Texas 77446

National Science Teachers Association
1742 Connecticut Avenue, N.W.
Washington, D.C. 20009

School Science and Mathematics Association
126 Life Science Bldg.
Bowling Green State University
Bowling Green, Ohio 43403

United Nations Environment Programme
P.O. Box 20
Grand Central Station
New York, N.Y. 10017

U.S. Department of Agriculture
Information Services Staff
Extension Service
Washington, D.C. 20250

The World of the Arts

"Developing values to guide her actions and to provide the foundation for sound decision-making"

— Girl Scout program emphasis

Activities in the World of the Arts include many opportunities for the Daisy Girl Scout to express herself through various art forms. She is able to re-create her perceptions of her world, to appreciate the beauty of the many arts in our world, to develop her talents, skills, gifts, and competence, and to share her experiences with others.

It is important to let each girl experience these activities in her own way within an environment of support and trust. The quality of the process of observing and creating art is what will most strongly affect her growth and development.

Daisy Girl Scouts need to experience art and the world through their senses. They need to learn that ideas and materials for art projects and activities can be found everywhere. The wind can create music. A leaf can be a perfect picture. A bit of yarn can become hair for a puppet or the perfect finishing touch for a collage. A hunk of wood can be a piece of sculpture. Letting Daisy Girl Scouts discover this develops their creativity and teaches them to use resources wisely.

Experiencing Sounds

You'll need:

1. Many objects and ways to make sounds with them. Be sure to have everyone participate in thinking of, and collecting, the materials.

Some objects are:

rattle	egg beater	horn
maracas	whistle	bell

Some sounds are:

a broom sweeping	paper crumpling
wood being sawed	a pencil being sharpened
a ball bouncing	
a foot stomping	dried beans being shaken in a can
hands clapping	
fingers snapping	a nail being hammered
water splashing	wood being sanded

There are also the sounds of:

teeth being brushed	whispering, yelling, crying, laughing
hair being combed	

2. A partition made with a sheet on a clothesline or moveable screen so the "soundmaker" will be out of the other players' view.

Give the girls time to experience the materials to see what kinds of sounds they can make with them. Then, let one girl go behind the screen and make different sounds with the materials while the others guess.

If a sound is not guessed correctly, the soundmaker should show the group the soundmaking in process.

Everyone who wishes to be a soundmaker should be able to have a turn.

BEYOND

With an adult's help (parents, leaders, etc.), children may make tape recordings of sounds in their environments and then play them back, to listen to, and identify, the sounds again.

Have a mystery smelling activity. The girls can bring in different foods to smell and then when blindfolded try to guess what each thing is (onions, vanilla, peppermint, bananas, peanut butter, garlic, melons, mangoes, etc.)

Have a mystery tasting activity. Girls bring in different foods to taste and try to identify them.

Identify items and textures by touch. Blindfolded girls can identify rough, smooth, wet, soft, granulated items. Girls can bring items to identify.

Music and Dramatics

Young children like to sing and dance and make believe. They sing for the love of it, for the sound of the melody and the sound of familiar words. They dance for the sheer joy of moving freely to a rhythm that is felt or heard.

There is no place in the Daisy Girl Scout program for formal performances, memorized lines, long rehearsals. What the girls do should be fun. Much of it will just happen. The remainder should be pleasantly learned and easy to remember.

Below are some suggested activities. You may wish to adapt ideas or add additional ones. Encourage girls to share songs they sing at home, to invent their own dances, and to act out their own stories.

Daisy Girl Scout Band

Keep this very simple. Some of the children may have had experience with a rhythm band. Let them suggest what instruments they would like in their Daisy Girl Scout band. The instruments can be homemade from materials around the house. Dried melon seeds inside a cardboard or plastic container make good shakers. Two smooth sticks can be rhythm sticks. Jingle bells like those used to decorate gift wraps can be attached to a pie plate to make a tambourine. Let the girls have the freedom to make any sounds they choose.

Instruments often used in rhythm bands include drums, rhythm sticks, bells, shakers, and tambourines.

Use the band to accompany singing, letting the girls decide which instruments go best with each song. Or use the instruments to sound out the rhythm of dancing or marching.

Perfection is not the goal; giving girls the chance to express themselves, to make choices, and to work together is.

Songs—for Dancing

Children can dance to almost any sound. "El Lobo—The Wolf," in *Skip to My Lou*, is a good song for dancing. As they become familiar with the tune, the girls can make up their own dance steps. Encourage them to move to the rhythm of the music in any song they sing.

Dramatizing Songs

Take the words of any song and let the children act them out. "Planting Rice," in *Skip to My Lou* and "El Tren" and "Mi Chacra" in *Canciones de Nuestra Cabaña* are good for dramatizing, as are many others in these songbooks.

Think of all the ways girls could act out "Make New Friends" in the *Brownies' Own Songbook*—two friends meeting on the street, a child visiting a family member, a little girl meeting a new neighbor. Let the girls use their imagination to make a story of any song they know.

Songs for Singing

Songs express many emotions. Quiet songs, or those often sung for ceremonies, include "Make New Friends" and "Taps," which you will find in *Sing Together*. The traditional Girl Guide/Girl Scout grace, "For Health and Strength," may be supplemented with graces suggested by parents and girls.

Some songs are fun to sing anytime, such as "We're All Together Again" and "Frog Round" from *Sing Together* and "Kookaburra" from *Canciones*. As girls are preparing to bridge into Brownie Girl Scouting, they will enjoy learning the "Brownie Smile Song," which you will find in the *Brownies' Own Songbook*.

It is best for Daisy Girl Scouts to sing in unison. As the girls progress in their singing ability, they will be able to sing many of these songs as rounds.

Not all children of Daisy Girl Scout age will be able to carry a tune. Some children do not learn to do this until the age of seven or eight. The main focus should be on their enjoyment of music and singing.

Reading Aloud

One of the best, easiest, and most satisfying activities you can choose is reading aloud. Hearing the language helps children learn to read. Read either short stories or longer ones in several parts, but be sure to know the book yourself before you share it with the girls. If the book has pictures, take time to have girls get comfortably settled where they can easily see the book as you read it.

Poems, like music, are meant to be heard. Read poetry aloud. You may feel a bit self-conscious at first, but you will find that children dearly love the sound of words, and they will be uncritical of your dramatic talents! You will find several resources listed, all of them readily available. You might start with these.

Butterfly of the air
how beautiful you are:
butterfly of the air
gilded and green
Light of the lamp
butterfly of the air,
stay there, there, there! . . .
You don't want to stop,
to stop you don't want.
Butterfly of the air
gilded and green
Light of the lamp,
butterfly of the air,
stay there, there, there! . . .
Stay there!
Butterfly, are you there?
　　　　—Federico Garcia Lorca, *"The Cricket Sings"*

The Prancing Pony

Your prancing, dancing pony—
Oh, please don't tie him here,
This cherry tree's in blossom—
Oh dear, dear, dear!

He'll prance and dance and whinny,
He'll neigh and stomp and call,
And down the soft, pink blossoms
Will fall, fall, fall!
　　　　—from *The Prancing Pony:
　　　　Nursery Rhymes from Japan*

Poem

I loved my friend.
He went away from me.
There's nothing more to say.
The poem ends,
Soft as it began—

I loved my friend.
　　　　—Langston Hughes, *Don't You Turn Back*

Hope

Sometimes when I'm lonely
Don't know why,
Keep thinkin' I won't be lonely
By and by
                    —Langston Hughes, *Don't You Turn Back*

Dressing

It would be easier, of course,
to dress like any cow or horse;

No zipping-up or zipping-down
or changing clothes to go to town,

No snapping-on or hooking-in
or itchy collars at your chin,

No putting-on or taking-off
or bundling-up to stop a cough,

It would be easier, of course,
but then, who'd BE a cow or horse?
                    —Aileen Fisher, *In One Door and Out the Other*

Spider

I saw a little spider
with the smartest spider head
She made . . . somewhere inside her . . .
a magic silken thread.

I saw her sliding down it.
She dangled in the air.
I saw her climbing up it
and pulling up each stair.

She made it look so easy
I wished all day I knew
how I could spin a magic thread
so I could dangle too.
                    —Aileen Fisher, *Cricket in the Thicket*

Jump or Jiggle

Frogs jump,
Caterpillars hump.

Worms wiggle,
Bugs jiggle.

Rabbits hop,
Horses clop.

Snakes slide,
Seagulls glide.

Mice creep,
Deer leap.

Puppies bounce,
Kittens pounce.

But . . .
I walk.
        —Lucy Sprague Mitchell, *Here and Now Story Book*

Storytelling

Storytelling is an excellent learning experience for children. It builds a love for and appreciation of language. It helps them use their imaginations, as they picture the story in their minds. And it helps them think things out when they're telling their own stories.

Tell stories and read stories to the girls. Many colorful, interesting books can be borrowed from children's libraries. (See lists in resources section.) Children like stories with action and repetition. Sometimes they ask for a favorite story over and over again.

Give the girls a chance to tell stories they have heard. It will be interesting to see how much they remember and how much they invent. Encourage them to act out scenes from the story.

Next, let them make up their own stories and act them out. Once in a while, write out a story told by a child and put her name on the paper. Each girl could dictate a story to an adult or older girl. Then

draw a picture to go with it. Some girls may rather do a picture story, asking a helper to write something under each picture. Each girl could take her story home, or the stories could be put together to make a Daisy Girl Scout storybook.

Use local folklore, stories you've heard or have been told, or make up your own stories, to tell children at storytelling time.

STORYTELLING TECHNIQUES
Be sure to know the story well, and tell it with interest and enthusiasm.

Use a tone of voice that follows the story. For example, soft tones for quiet scenes, lighthearted tones for happy scenes.

Practice telling the story to someone before you tell it to the girls.

Use pictures or hand motions to illustrate the action.

Encourage your troop to tell stories to one another and to be both good listeners and interesting tellers.

Acting Without Words

Acting without talking—pantomime—is another way to help heighten a child's imagination. Do simple things that don't take preparation. Here are a few examples:

- Walk across the room very quietly as if a baby is sleeping.
- Walk as if you are very angry.
- Walk as if the wind is blowing hard.
- Walk as if you are happy.
- Try to look sad.
- Try to look as if you just spilled a glass of milk.
- Look as if you are hiding.
- Pretend you are picking up a heavy pail of water and handing it to someone.
- Pretend you are picking up a needle and handing it to someone.

If girls like these activities, they may be ready to act out small scenes in pantomime. With three or four in each group, the girls should decide on something to act with the others as audience. The audience tries to guess what happened in the scene. Girls may need simple ideas to start. Once they get the idea, it can be fun. But if the actors or the spectators don't seem to be enjoying themselves, change quickly to another activity.

Creative Interpretation

These activities help Daisy Girl Scouts gain confidence and skill in the use of their bodies, as well as giving them chances to use their imagination and creativity.

This is an activity that the girls will enjoy, and one that needs no equipment, no props—nothing but imagination. It's a game of let's pretend.

Pretend we're walking barefoot:

on really hot pavement	on a straight tightrope
through a muddy puddle	in chocolate pudding
	over a slippery floor
on sharp rocks	

Be:

as small as you can	wind
as wide as you can	rain
water	a butterfly

Pretend to eat:

an apple	a caramel apple
a melting ice-cream cone	very hot soup
	a sour pickle

Make up your own.

Costume Box

Girls of this age are still very good at pretending, so costumes are not always necessary. However, it is fun sometimes to make simple costumes with whatever is at hand. Old newspapers cut to size and pinned to girls' clothes make wonderful temporary costumes. Pieces of cloth, clothing no longer used, and even rags have possibilities.

Don't worry about details. The girls can decide on their costumes. Giving them a chance to create something is much more important than having "correct" costumes. When they are older, they can learn about formal dramatics and proper costumes. Some troops save odds and ends from costumes and keep them in a costume box. Friends, sponsors, program consultants, and the girls' own families can all contribute to the costume box. Once in a while, girls may just want to "dress up" and pretend they are other people!

Puppets

Often a shy child will feel more at ease speaking behind a puppet. She can pretend that the puppet, not she, is talking or singing. Use puppets for telling stories, for simple playacting, or for songs and recitations. Make puppets to tell a story. Let the girls decide the characters they need. Keep the puppets very simple.

In a way, working with puppets is the opposite of pantomime where girls are seen and not heard. With puppets, children are heard but not seen. In playacting, girls are both seen and heard. Try to give girls a chance to experiment with all three. Then let them do what they seem to enjoy most.

Paper Cup Puppets

Use small paper cups, squares of tissue, or cloth, felt markers, bits of paper or yarn. Cut a hole in the side of the cup, so a finger can poke out for the nose. Add paper strips for hair, or use yarn. Ears can be added for animals. Make a face with drops of glue (if cup has waxy surface, rub with soapy cloth first). Make two holes in tissue or cloth for fingers.

Lollipop Puppets

Lollipop puppets are easy. Start with a paper plate. Girls draw a face for the role they plan to play. They can use odds and ends to make hair, scarves, and glue or tape a stick to the back of the plate. To act out a puppet show, each girl puts the lollipop puppet in front of her face.

103

Peanut Finger Puppets

Break peanut shells in half so that they fit over a finger like a thimble. Daisy Girl Scouts may want to make any number from one to five puppets. They can put a face on each puppet with a marking pen and use yarn or string for hair. Girls then place the shells on their fingers and make conversations with the puppets on other girls' fingers.

Cardboard Puppets

Draw a head or a whole character on a piece of stiff cardboard. Attach a long, stiff piece of cardboard to the back as a handle so the puppet can be moved about.

Potato Puppets

Let each girl scoop out enough of her potato so she can put her index finger in to hold it up. Then help her drape "clothes" around her closed fist. She can decorate the top of the potato to make a face.

Other items for making puppets include socks, stockings, gloves, paper bags, dried apples, and dried corn cobs.

The Visual Arts

For five-year-olds, the visual arts include drawing and painting, prints, constructions, embroidery, sculpture, and even toys and games. They enjoy working with clay, finger paints, wood, and paper. Daisy Girl Scouts need to experiment with as many different art materials as possible; later they will learn technique and how-to's. Their artwork is largely symbolic. They use color, shape, and line in ways that give their paintings, drawings, and constructions the look of modern art rather than realism. If a body has no arms and is mostly head, and an animal is purple and green, that is fine. The creativity and uninhibited self-expression of Daisy Girl Scouts should be encouraged in their visual arts activities.

The young child most naturally chooses to express herself in arts that relate directly to her world—her home, relatives, pets, school, trips she takes, etc. Usually, a girl of this age does not plan arrangements, but places things in pictures according to their present importance to her. Trips, books, and films enlarge her frame of reference by providing new stimuli.

Levels of Artistic Expression

Children pass through progressive developmental levels in expressing themselves artistically. The Daisy Girl Scouts in your troop might be:

AT LEVEL ONE
Line: Daisy Girl Scouts draw and paint simple forms, such as scribbles or masses of lines; later they tend toward spiral or circular lines. They usually depict people with large circular heads. Features may or may not be indicated, and arms and legs, with or without hands and feet, are often attached to the head.

Depth: Daisy Girl Scouts draw and paint figures without depicting a setting. They usually have very little sense of the proportions of the objects in their pictures.

Color: Daisy Girl Scouts like to experiment with color, creating their own color schemes, and painting with little regard to realism in color.

Texture: The first stage of learning about texture is through experimentation.

AT LEVEL TWO

Line: Daisy Girl Scouts draw or paint separate shapes, tending toward circular forms, which they see as animals, trees, flowers, clouds, people. They develop their own patterns for the human figure and generally use lines to indicate the ground and the sky; only later does the sky come all the way to the ground in their pictures.

Depth: At this stage, Daisy Girl Scouts draw things in the proportions that they feel them, rather than in the proportions that adults see them. Each form is placed in its own space without overlapping.

Color: Experiments with color continue. Daisy Girl Scouts now make secondary colors by combining two primary colors and begin to use blended colors. Gradually they begin to notice colors around them and paint with more regard for realism.

Texture: This stage usually sees the girls using strokes, patterns, and repeated forms and colors to create impressions of texture.

Experimenting with Line, Color, Texture, and Depth

During the art experiences they enjoy in the troop, your Daisy Girl Scouts learn to manipulate pencils, pens, brushes, and crayons through experimentation. They need to explore what these tools will do.

Line: Daisy Girl Scouts will use their imaginations to see different kinds of lines as pictures—a squiggly line becomes a worm, straight lines turn into a house, and curved lines become the sun. They have preconceived notions. The sky is often depicted as a straight line across the top of a picture, and the scene is firmly anchored by a sturdy base line. As they become more aware of details around them, the contents of their pictures will change.

Color: In the early stages of art activities, the girls will be more concerned with the way colors look in their paintings than whether they resemble the actual colors of the objects they are representing. Do not expect their colors to be realistic. After they have learned about primary and secondary colors, you can help them experiment with different values and intensities. Encourage them to observe the colors in nature, and they will begin to use that range of color in their paintings.

Texture: Daisy Girl Scouts observe the different kinds of textures on surfaces around them—smooth, rough, shiny, dull, even, and uneven. Ask the girls to collect things that have different textures and bring them to the meeting. The girls can then get a sense of what textures look like and how they feel.

Depth: Daisy Girl Scouts do not see depth as adults do. Further, everything has its own space. They determine size by the importance of objects or figures in their own worlds.

Art should teach the girls to think, observe, meet new problems, try different solutions, and express their feelings, thoughts, dreams, visions, and perceptions.

Tempera Painting

Tempera is a basic art medium in which Daisy Girl Scouts can express themselves freely. The painting can be done on an easel, on the floor, or on tables. All the girls should be encouraged, and given adequate time, to paint their own experiences and expressions. Since large bodily movements are characteristic of Daisy Girl Scouts, large brushes and large sheets of paper should be made available. For the young child who cannot express herself in writing, communicating through pictures is very important. Her pictures help her tell a story. You can help a five-year-old improve language skills by lettering the word or title of her picture under it. This helps her associate her own picture with a word.

Here are some procedures for using tempera:

1. Select good, clear, bright colors. Daisy Girl Scouts cannot be expected to know how to blend colors.

They generally tend to choose bright, primary colors, but you can help them learn how colors blend after they have mixed something themselves. You can then point out that a new color has been made by mixing two others. For example, red and blue make purple.

2. Mix paints to creamy consistency. Liquid paint can be stored in plastic squeeze bottles; powdered paint can be mixed to the consistency of thick frosting and stored in a tightly closed jar.

3. Cover the painting surface with several pieces of newspaper.

4. Have a brush for each color to keep colors clean.

5. Show children how to tap out excess paint in the brush on edge of a bottle or jar before painting.

6. Encourage children to experiment with tools other than a brush, such as a sponge. Brush paint over sponge and press sponge onto paper.

7. Discourage "scrubbing" action with a brush.

MATERIALS AND EQUIPMENT
You will need:

easels (if possible)	newsprint
liquid or powdered tempera	paint rags
brushes with ¾" bristles and long handles	smocks
	sponges measuring about 2 by 2 inches
a few watercolor brushes for detail only	newspaper
paper measuring at least 18 by 24 inches	

Paint can be put in small baby food jars for individual use, or use divided aluminum food plates or cupcake pans for palettes. Use only small amounts of paint at one time as it dries up after one day's use.

Cleaning up is part of painting. Time should be left for the cleanup process, and girls should be encouraged to learn how to clean brushes and palettes properly.

Finger Painting

Finger painting is the process of creating a picture or design using fingers, hands, and even parts of the arm to apply paint on a glazed piece of paper.

Finger paint is a delightfully messy art medium and should be great fun in the proper setting, but don't try it on your living room rug. Choose large tables with access to a sink, or a place where large cans or buckets of water are near worktables. Finger painting is a good activity for an outdoor meeting on picnic tables. This medium lends itself to freedom of movement and expression. Most girls have no trouble "feeling" the rhythm and movement the medium allows. It should be a joyful experience for Daisy Girl Scouts and produce great feelings of self-confidence.

MATERIALS AND EQUIPMENT
You will need:

finger paint or liquid starch and powdered tempera	bucket or large can for water
	washable tables
finger paint paper (glazed on working side)	aprons or smocks
sheets of newspaper	articles such as tongue depressors or combs to produce variations in design
paper towels	
sponge	

If the table is not washable, cover it completely with newspaper. A dab of starch under each corner of the finger-paint paper will anchor it to the newspaper and keep it from sliding around. Pick up newspaper and all to set aside for drying. Apply water to glazed side of paper with wet sponge. Smooth out wrinkles with sponge.

Place approximately a tablespoon of finger paint or mixture of liquid starch and powdered tempera in center of each paper. Girls should then spread out the paint over the entire surface of the paper with the flat of their hands. Allow children to choose their own colors and experiment. They will learn from experimentation how to keep colors from "muddying" together.

Encourage use of hands, arms, wrists, as well as fingers, fingernails, and tools such as notched cardboard, combs, sponges, etc.

Allow plenty of time for experimentation.

The picture can be erased by smoothing it out after each experiment. More water and paint can be added when desired. When final design is created, remove the painting to the drying area for several hours.

Hints: Have clean water and sponge close by. Encourage girls to wipe off their arms with sponge after each experiment. Have paper towels and wastebasket close at hand. Finger painting is best accomplished in a space large enough so that the girls can stand and move around the tables.

Crayon

Often the first art material a girl uses is a crayon. Although they too often are used to fill in other people's designs in coloring books, crayons can be a creative medium.

You can use large primary crayons, rounded crayons or crayons with points, broken unwrapped pieces, or flat pieces. Paper can be manila, measuring at least 12 by 18 inches, or 18 by 24-inch newsprint, or white drawing paper.

Let girls experiment with large crayons to learn the possibilities of using the point, the side, even pressure, uneven pressure.

Girls can experiment with flat crayons using strokes, curves, many small strokes, even drawing, and solid lines.

Hints: Encourage the girls to make bright drawings with strong colors. Let them experiment with pressure on the crayon—pressing hard, but not so hard that the crayon breaks. They can try colors next to each other, then overlapping colors to see the mixtures that colors make.

CRAYON TECHNIQUES

Crayon Resist

Have the girls draw a picture with crayon and fill in with bright colors, leaving some areas of the background uncolored. Then they can apply a thin coat of tempera over the entire picture. If the crayon has been applied heavily enough, the tempera will be repelled by the crayon areas and will adhere to the uncolored areas, creating an interesting textured picture.

Crayon Etching

The girls color the entire surface of paper with many colors of crayon. Pressing firmly, they make colors bright and solid. The whole surface of the picture is then painted with black, slightly thick, tempera or India ink. Or black crayon can be applied. With a pointed tool such as a nail file, the girls can then outline and scratch the details of an etching.

Hint: Pat chalk dust from chalkboard eraser over colored crayon design—it makes the top layer adhere.

Crayon Rubbings

Start with a coin, then look for other textures to create rubbing designs. Have the girls hold lightweight paper (such as typing paper) over coin and rub carefully with side of crayon. The design will show up in relief.

Lettering

The crayon is an excellent tool to start first experiments in lettering. Drawings with a word underneath can be first steps to reading and writing.

Drawing with Pencil and Marker

Sometimes children of this age love to draw very precise, detailed, linear pictures. If you have such a girl in your troop, by all means let her do her drawings. They will be filled with wonderful details she has observed in her daily life, but do not expect them to be realistic. Girls can use newsprint or drawing paper, soft pencils or felt pen for their pictures. If you give the girls markers to introduce color, make sure they are the watercolor kind.

Prints

Using very simple materials, it is possible to teach Daisy Girl Scouts the fundamentals of making prints.

You will need:

potatoes and carrots	flat brush to apply colors
tempera or poster paints	newspapers to cover table surface
absorbent paper, like typing paper, newsprint or even cardboard shirt backs	jar of water nearby
	smocks or aprons
	paper towels

PROCESS

1. Before the troop meets, peel and clean a few potatoes thoroughly. Put them in water to keep them from turning brown. Cut potatoes in half and place flat surface down on paper towel until ready to print. Potatoes are watery and will give a blurred print if you try to use them immediately after cutting. Have a few carrots available to cut in sections.

2. Have paints and paper on tables, ready to go.

3. Cut the potato halves in the shape of your design. Squares, triangles, and rectangles are usually enough variation for Daisy Girl Scouts. The stamp will give several impressions but will not last indefinitely. You need a separate potato stamp for each color, because the potato is porous and retains the color. Use the carrots for circle designs.

4. To print, the brush is dipped into the paint and the flat area of the potato or carrot stamp is covered with color. The painted side is then pressed firmly onto the paper to be printed.

HINTS

This type of printing helps the girls see the possibilities in relief printing. When they get older, they can transfer this learning to more complicated designs in eraser or linoleum prints. Help them see the design possibilities in repeating a pattern. The same shape turned different ways creates many designs; an overall design can be made for wrapping paper. Greeting cards can be made by using a border design or one design in the corner. Try the same shape in different colors as an overall pattern and experiment with the many possibilities.

Thumbprints

This is a good experiment that requires just fingers, paint, paper, and a pencil, and demonstrates how a print is made.

Even strokes of color are painted over a thumb or finger, which then is pressed carefully on paper without blurring. Girls may need to experiment until they get the right amount of paint. Ask them to "imagine" what the shapes are like and draw additions to the thumbprint. Let them try antlers, tails, legs, or feelers to create whatever they see in the prints. A stamp pad can also be used for these prints, but make sure it has washable ink.

Collage

Collage is the art of creating a picture or composition by gluing various materials (paper, cloth, wood, etc.) to a sheet of paper. Sometimes a drawing or color accents are added. This process is excellent for developing creative attributes. Looking for materials, making choices among them, and arranging and rearranging them challenges girls to combine various elements into a new whole. Help when a girl needs encouragement or when she has trouble gluing pieces down on the background. There are really no right and wrong answers in collage.

MATERIALS
You will need:

a scrap box with sewing basket scraps (cloth, rickrack, buttons, lace), small scraps of wool, old playing cards, old railroad or theater tickets, postcards, gift wrapping, greeting cards, magazines, dry leaves, twigs, acorns, small interesting pebbles, small shells, etc.

white glue in plastic squeeze bottles

paper for background (13 by 18 inches or larger)—manila, tagboard, clipboard

scissors

paints and brushes or markers

stapler

HINTS
Have plenty of materials available to allow for choices, and keep replenishing the scrap box. Motivate a game to hunt for more materials. Discuss the materials, and help girls imagine what they might turn into. Discuss combining smooth and rough textures. Demonstrate how to glue materials. Allow suitable time to work; collage takes time.

Make Collections

Collecting helps build a girl's curiosity and thinking skills in categorizing, naming, observing, and using things. These are some items the girls might collect. They will think of others.

nails	sugar packets
autographs	corks
buttons	marbles
shells	fabric swatches
rocks	keys
screws	leaves
nuts and bolts	dried flowers
beads	labels
bottle caps	drinking straw wrappers
coins	

The girls can choose different things to collect. They can then share or trade. Help them devise ways of mounting or keeping their collections. Egg cartons are especially useful.

Stitchery

Stitchery combines the elements of picture-making and design with experiences of manipulating materials of various textures, sizes, and types. The process of placing the decorative stitches and choosing and combining materials offers many creative possibilities for children of all ages. Daisy Girl Scouts can learn to do various stitchery designs. They should treat their stitchery as a painting or collage and not feel the necessity to learn specific stitches.

An initial step could be the search for materials. The girls could be asked to bring in pieces of yarn, ribbon, strings, and thread. The collection can be looked over and discussed. Then you can give each girl a small piece of fabric (burlap is best to start), a large needle, and yarn.

Ask: What can we do with these yarns? Who can think of a stitch to make? How can you make a long line? The girls will learn the possibilities and the limitations of the materials and will then be ready to move on to larger pieces.

MATERIALS AND EQUIPMENT
You will need:

cloth for base—linen, cotton, wool, burlap, or other fabrics that are loosely woven, in various textures and colors

Appliqué materials—beads, buttons, cloth scraps, lace, rickrack, etc.

needles—blunt steel (#13 tapestry needle) or plastic needle

scissors

frame to hold base cloth

HINTS
A frame is a useful piece of equipment to have, although not absolutely essential. It does help stretch the material to make it easier to work on. Embroidery hoops may be used, but old frames—discarded picture frames, used needlepoint frames, etc.—would be less expensive. Let each girl choose background material. Staple or tack it to the frame, stretching evenly.

Help the girls plan the design so that there are large working areas. Avoid fine details. Select and lay out materials and pieces to be added on background before sewing.

Encourage the use of different kinds of stitches—to appliqué materials; to create forms, shapes, and backgrounds; to vary textures and colors. If a girl asks for help in learning a certain stitch, show her, but otherwise let her make up her own stitches.

A next step is a group project. Create a wall-hanging, a banner, or a mural. In these projects, each girl should play a part in the design so that the group project has meaning for all of them.

FINISHING PIECES FOR DISPLAY
Machine stitch edges of small or lightweight fabrics to prevent raveling, or fringe edges.

You can also hang lightweight pieces by sewing wide hems at the top and bottom edges and inserting dowels in flaps.

Heavier pieces can be lined and metal rings or loops used for hangers.

Pieces may also be framed on stretchers.

Three-Dimensional Arts

In addition to enjoying the "flat" visual arts of drawing and painting, young children need to work with three-dimensional materials. These help them relate form to space and allow them to see their artwork from several angles.

Clay

Clay is an excellent material for Daisy Girl Scouts to work with. It is worked a little like bread dough, by kneading and rounding and rolling. It is a pliable, inexpensive, reusable modeling material that can be purchased wet or dry and stored in a plastic bag closed with a clothespin. Glazing can be done at a local high school or craft school. Self-hardening clay is another choice, since it does not have to be fired.

You will need:

enough clay to give each child a large ball

pieces of plastic to cover tables

an old wooden board

rolling pin

pot of water nearby

aprons or smocks

some orange sticks, screws, and miscellaneous objects to make designs on the clay.

Keep the projects simple. Let the girls roll, press, and pinch the clay to create weed holders, simple animals, or pinch pots. They can make a weed holder by rolling the clay flat and making holes in it with a toothpick. Let the weed holder dry and have it fired. Then have an expedition and gather weeds to dry for the holder. The girls can also experiment by adding texture to a flat slab of clay, creating designs on it with an orange stick. A hole, made at the top before the slab dries, can turn the slab into a decorative plaque.

Cleanup is part of the process of using clay. Hands should be washed, clay picked up and stored in plastic bags. Remind the girls not to throw water with clay pieces in it down a sink.

If you do not have access to clay, use one of these clay dough recipes:

Salt Dough Clay

6 cups flour

2 cups salt

1/4 cup vegetable oil

2 cups water

food coloring as desired

Mix flour and salt first. Mix liquids together and add to dry mixture. Blend with hands. Add more oil and water if needed. Store in airtight container.

Baker's Dough

4 cups flour

1 cup salt

1 1/2 cups water (1/4 cup more if needed)

Mix thoroughly with hands. Knead five minutes. After recipe is made, children can shape the clay into animals, people, ornaments, etc. Put them on a cookie sheet. Bake for one hour at 350 degrees.

You can expand upon the things the girls learn about modeling by showing them some clay objects made by artists. Visit an exhibit at a local crafts fair, school, or museum.

Constructions

WOOD

Learning to use tools is one of the benefits of working with scraps of wood at this age. Little girls can learn to saw and use a hammer and nails just as well as little boys.

You will need:

pieces of wood (can be leftovers from projects children's families may be doing, or scraps from lumberyard)	hammer
	flathead nails
	sandpaper
some 2-inch × 4-inch pine, long enough to saw	C-clamp or vise to hold pieces of wood for sawing
other soft wood pieces	white glue
crosscut saw	

Use real tools, not miniature toys. By working in pairs, and with proper supervision, girls can learn to handle these tools properly and safely.

For Daisy Girl Scouts, actually building something with wood is not important. Just the process of sawing and hammering nails into pieces of wood is worthwhile. If you have a variety of sizes and shapes of wood, you also could help the girls make some creative constructions. Do not try to build anything specific; just assemble pieces by nailing or gluing them together. Girls' imaginations will create sculpturelike assemblages. Learning to sand a piece of wood, to take off the rough edges, is also a good activity in conjunction with woodwork.

ICE CREAM STICK CONSTRUCTIONS

If you cannot find wood scraps, you can still do three-dimensional constructions with ice-cream sticks, coffee stirrers, and tongue depressors. Use white glue to hold pieces in place. Spread newspapers over table surface. Use other scraps to add variety to the materials. Girls should work together in pairs, as the process needs hands to hold the pieces in place until the glue sets.

Other Sources of Information

American Alliance for Health, Physical Education,
  and Dance (AAHPERD)
1900 Association Drive
Reston, Va. 22091

American Alliance for Theatre and Education
Theatre Arts Department
Virginia Tech.
Blacksburg, Va. 24061

American Craft Council
40 West 53rd Street
New York, N.Y. 10019

American Council for the Arts
3rd Floor, Area M
1285 Avenue of the Americas
New York, N.Y. 10019

American Music Conference
303 East Wacker Drive, Suite 1214
Chicago, Ill. 60601

American Theatre Arts for Youth
1429 Walnut Street
Philadelphia, Pa. 19102

Music Educators National Conference
1902 Association Drive
Reston, Va. 22091

Music Teachers National Association
441 Vine Street, Suite 2113
Cincinnati, Ohio 45202

National Art Education Association
1916 Association Drive
Reston, Va. 22091

Very Special Arts (Disabled)
Education Office
John F. Kennedy Center for the Performing Arts
Washington, D.C. 20566

The World of the Out-of-Doors

"...to protect and improve the world around me..."

—Girl Scout Law

Daisy Girl Scouts belong in the outdoors—their own outdoors. They need to run, to play, to feel and roll and smell, to look and shout and listen. Plan as many activities as possible for outside the meeting place. Hold meetings in the backyard; borrow a neighbor's garden for an hour; use a patio, a porch, a small corner of the schoolyard, a bit of a neighborhood park. Explore a vacant lot, a patch of weeds, a window box. Take a walk in the rain or the snow.

As you lead the girls in their outdoor experiences, it is important to relax and enjoy your time together in the out-of-doors. Listen to their questions and comments. Observe them as they learn about nature and the outdoor world. Share observations, discoveries, thoughts, and feelings with them. Let them use their bodies and senses to learn. They need to experience the out-of-doors directly. Just talking to them about it is not enough.

A wide variety of outdoor experiences, a continuing exploration of the natural environment, and an appreciation of the human environment can all be part of the troop's activities.

Walk Outside

Built Environment

Take a short walk with the girls, have them look at the buildings. Ask if they are old or new, high or low? Which one has the most windows? What are the buildings made of?

Box Block

Help the girls build a block out of boxes. Use milk cartons, cereal cartons, etc. Ask them to identify some of the buildings they saw.

Be What You See

Have the girls look for animals. Big ones. Little ones. Were some of them pets? How about insects?

The girls can act out an insect, or a bird, or any animal they saw. Ask them if a caterpillar moves the same way as a butterfly. Do birds walk like people? Let them show the difference.

Trees and Leaves

Organize a walk to look for plants, trees. Ask them to think about shapes. Are the trees round, skinny, top-heavy, smooth, rough? Who lives in the tree? Under it? Were there any shrubs? Were the leaves all the same? Did any of the leaves smell good?

Ask the girls to pick just one leaf each off the ground. Have them tape their leaves on a piece of paper, and look at them very carefully. They can press a leaf that has heavy veins into a flat piece of clay. When they pull the leaf carefully away, they will have a leaf print.

Framing the Picture

Have the girls make their very own picture frame to frame the world by tearing the middle out of a 3″ by 5″ card or a scrap of construction paper. If you don't want them to tear the papers, you can pre-cut them before your experience. Have the girls hold the frames at arms-length. How much of the world can they see? Can they find a beautiful picture to share with someone else? Have them hold the frame close to their eyes. What do they see when they get down to the ground? Talk about things that are seen up close and things that are seen far away. You should be able to frame "micro" (small) and "macro" (large) pictures with your frames.

Nature Lotto

This actually involves several activities, both of which can be very elaborate or very simple, depending upon how you approach them. The preparation portion can be done beforehand by the leader or older Girl Scouts, or can be part of a Daisy Girl Scout meeting as a way of planning for the actual interaction with the Lotto Cards.

The object is to make "lotto" cards showing common objects and living creatures that can be found by the girls on a hike out-of-doors. You can make each girl a card, make the same card for everyone, make cards that are different for teams, or everyone can share the same card. See illustration.

Materials for this project vary, and you can use an approach best suited to your needs.

Suggestions for construction:

cardboard, tagboard, or heavy paper to form the lotto board.

small pictures of plants, animals, natural objects and man-made objects you are liable to encounter on your walk. These can be collected from old magazines, used books from rummage sales, coloring books, stickers, nature center brochures, illustrations done by girls or yourself.

glue to glue pictures down.

clear contact paper to cover boards with.

It helps to predraw lines on your cardboard or heavy paper so that you can paste your pictures in the boxes formed. It is up to you as to how many lotto spaces you create.

Suggested topics for board squares might include an ant, a butterfly, a caterpillar, several birds specific to your area, evergreen or deciduous trees, rock, soil, shells, snails, slugs, lizards, squirrels, deer, dead leaves, worms, mushrooms, flowers, specific buildings, statues, etc.

The finished lotto board is a great tool for an exploratory hike in the neighborhood, a park, or the forest. You can make your lotto board specific to the site you will be visiting by a pre-visit or contacting people who are familiar with the area. The lotto game should not be competitive, but encourage observation skills and discussion about familiar and unfamiliar objects.

Growing Things

Growing something can be an exciting and rewarding experience for the girls.

Roots and Seeds

There are many possible containers. Margarine tubs, cottage cheese cartons, egg cartons, plastic drinking cups can all be used. Be sure to poke a small hole, or holes, in all of them so that the water can drain. Let girls mix some soil. Use garden soil and potting soil. Have them fill the containers, pat down, and then plant:

apple, orange, grapefruit, watermelon seeds saved from eaten fruit

beans or lima beans, which grow quickly and are interesting to watch

wheat, which grows very quickly into green lawn

Try suspending carrots, beets, radishes, turnips in water on toothpicks, also sweet potatoes. Or just grow the tops in water on pebbles. Be careful with turnips. Sometimes they rot and smell.

The girls can plant birdseed and see what comes up. If you start with a good mixture, you may end up with an interesting little forest. Some birdseed, however, is infertile. So be sure to check with a resource person.

Flower bulbs (tulips, crocuses, etc.) are fun to plant in the fall, so your troop can watch them come up in the spring.

Corn, Beans, and Squash

Another interesting activity is to plant beans, squash, and corn in the same pot or plot. Many American Indians used this method of planting. The corn grows up, the beans grow around the corn, and the squash grows down at the bottom providing good shade for the soil. You'll need:

large planting pot (around 18 inches deep and wide)

a whole fish (preferably fresh) 4 to 6 inches long, or a fish head

soil

corn, squash, and green bean seeds

Fill the pot half-full with the soil, and place the fish or fish head flat in the pot. Cover the fish with about three to four inches more soil. Put the seeds in together (a few of each). Then cover the seeds

with four to six inches more soil (check planting measurement on seed packages). Keep moist. Give lots of sun when the shoots start to come up. When the plants start to grow, the girls will see how the bean grows around the corn as it grows up, and how the squash grows out around the bottom, protecting the soil.

Harvest Time Fun

A trip to the country, a neighbor's backyard, a city park, or public garden when fruit or vegetables are ripe can be an adventure for the girls. Find the proper person to contact for permission to visit the site and pick items for your harvest-time project. While you are at the site, have the girls discover the needs of the particular crop. You may be looking at a commercially-run orchard or a backyard apple tree. You might discuss the kinds of jobs generated by such a harvest from the field to the grocery store.

Here are some ideas that you can build upon:

Visit a pumpkin patch in the fall and make jack-o-lanterns for Halloween as a group project, or make individual tart-size pumpkin pies.

Visit an apple orchard or an apple tree and pick apples to make apple cider, baked apples, apple-sauce, or apple juice. If you have access to an old-fashioned cider press in your community, this is a fun process for girls to be involved in. Otherwise, a home blender, along with strainers, can do a good job.

Pick other fruits and experiment with making natural juices. Try such fruits as grapes, pears, berries, tomatoes, oranges, or guavas.

To involve girls in the juice-making process, have them wash fruit, help with peeling (if necessary), run the blender, transfer pulp to the strainer, and use cloth or wire strainers. Caution is urged if girls are handling knives. Many Daisy Girl Scouts are not able to do this safely, and all should be supervised on a one-on-one basis.

117

Getting to Know Nature

Rocks

Rocks provide girls with an opportunity to explore size, shape, texture, and color. Each rock has individual characteristics.

To begin, play outdoors. Tell the group that each girl has five minutes to go and find as many rocks as she can. When time is up, sit down and talk about the rocks. Do any two look alike? Are there different colors? Do they feel different? Which is heavier?

The group might then sort the rocks into kinds: color, textures, shapes, etc.

Temperature

With the girls, explore a hot/cold day. Is it just as hot/cold everywhere? Show them how to read a thermometer. Take readings out in the sun, in the shade, in the grass, under a bush, on the pavement or a cement walk. Have the girls discuss why some places are cooler/hotter than others. Relate this to wildlife. How does the heat/cold affect plants and animals? What grows and lives in the different places?

Walk through the Year

When your troop first begins to meet, choose a specific walk or hike to make several times during the year. Observe the changes as the year progresses. After the hike, have the girls share what they noticed. They could make paintings, write, dictate, or tell stories or poems about their observations.

Leaf Prints

Have the girls pick up leaves from different trees off the ground and arrange them flat on a table in a collage. They can put a piece of paper over the leaves and, with crayons, rub back and forth on the paper. The pattern of the leaves will start to appear on the paper.

Another type of leaf print may be done by placing a leaf or leaves on paper. A fine wire screen is held over the paper, and the paint brush rubbed across it. The paint will spatter on the leaf and paper. When the leaf is removed, its shape will be outlined on the paper by the spattered paint.

Have the girls get to know a tree (or each girl can pick her own tree) and find out as much as they can about it—how it feels, what kind it is. Let them listen to its sap running upward in the early spring, hug it, see how it changes through the seasons, and observe what the leaves are like through the year.

Challenge Course

Have the girls design a challenge course with different things in their environment (trees, tires, bushes, fences, chairs, swings). Let them decide how the course will be run and then learn the course. After they know it, some may like to be timed with a stopwatch to see if they can beat their own record. Example: they may want to run around a tree, through a tire, around a bush, under an open fence, sit on a chair, swing twice on a swing, and run back to their starting place.

Animals

Have the girls tell what kinds of pets or other animals are at home or nearby—dogs, cats, horses, cows, rabbits, goats, and also ants, bees, birds. Ask them what these animals eat. How do they sleep? Do any of them sleep standing up?

Talk about how animals protect themselves from danger. Some have claws, hoofs, stingers, teeth, sharp beaks. Some can run very fast or hide very well.

Discuss how you should act around any unfamiliar animal. Discuss the differences between domestic and wild animals. Talk about why you do not feed wildlife in zoos or in the wild. Many animals can not digest the food they are given (gum in the wild will kill many animals) or will come to depend upon handouts or garbage around places where people visit or camp. If birds are adopted for the winter, they should continue to be fed until they can find food on their own.

Find Animal Homes

See how many animal homes the girls can find on a short walk in the neighborhood or in a park. Look for spider webs, bird nests, doghouses, stables, gopher holes, anthills, and others. Provide opportunities to interact with animals in safe settings. Visit someone's cat, dog, horse, guinea pig, hamster, bird, fish. Encourage girls to observe how the animal eats, moves, looks, feels, sounds. Let them talk to the owner to find out answers to questions they may have about the pet. Then visit a nature center or zoo. Let the girls talk to the zookeeper or a zoo staff person who knows about the animals.

Camouflage

Cover your eyes for five minutes while the girls hide. They must try to camouflage themselves, but they must be able to see you from their hiding places. After five minutes, give the girls a signal and uncover your eyes. The girls have to try and stay still and blend into the environment while you try to spot as many players as you can. You must stay in your position while spotting the hiders, but you may turn around to look for them. After you spot as many players as you can, by pointing and calling their names, another person may take your place.

Imitate Nature

Have girls tell something about land, rocks, trees. Have them pretend they are a tree, a rock, a blade of grass, a soft cloud, the warm sun, a butterfly, an ant, a worm, a bird. Ask them how they would position their body, how they would move it. Each girl might take a turn and let everyone try to guess what she is.

Sounds

Listen to the sounds in nature—birds, branches, leaves, frogs, bees, wind, falling water, ocean waves, gulls, and other animals. If a large seashell is available, let each girl hold it up to her ear. What does it sound like? Help girls concentrate on listening to sounds in their natural environment. Let them tell others what they hear. Talking about sound helps them think and learn.

Weather Calendar

On each meeting day, discuss the weather. Write the weather condition on the calendar for that date.

Discuss the meaning of such words as sunny, cold, warm, rainy, cloudy, foggy, windy. Look for designs and shapes in clouds.

Twig Creatures

Take a hike and help the girls find some "twig creatures," or any other nature objects such as a piece of bark, a rock that resembles an insect, a bird, or an animal.

Touch and Feel

Make a "touch and feel box" by cutting a doorway in the side of a shoe box through which small hands will fit. Staple a "curtain" over the doorway. Put several different nature items in the box. Replace the cover. Let girls reach in to guess what they are touching and feeling. Let them know that the objects in the box will not hurt them.

or

Make two identical "touch bags," one for each hand. Let the girls reach in and try to bring out matching objects.

Sounds 'n' Scents

Designate a certain large area, all of which you can observe, such as a yard. Divide the girls into two groups. With each group starting at the same point, one group moves in a clockwise circle, the other in a wider counterclockwise circle. One group tells all the different sounds they hear. The other group tells all the different scents they smell.

Alphabet Hike

On the hike, a girl who sees something beginning with the letter "A" that pertains to nature, names it. Then the girls look for something that begins with the letter "B," and so on through the alphabet.

Number Hike

On the hike, a girl sees one of something and names it, then another sees two of something and names them, three of, four of . . .

Bug Watch

Have the girls find an insect that they can watch. Have them watch for movements, food sources, methods of communication, and how distances are traveled. Have the girls look for camouflaging techniques. If possible, let the girls observe the insect through a hand lens or magnifying glass. Watch out for insects that sting or bite. Girls can act out insect behavior or draw what they have seen.

Under the Board

All sorts of wriggly creatures can be found under rotten logs, old boards, or bricks, in the city or country. Know the area that you are in so that you do not tangle with snakes or scorpions, and use an old pair of shoes or a shovel to help lift up objects that have been stationary for some time in backyards or vacant lots. Ask the girls if they think they will find anything before exposing creatures that need dark and damp places.

Talk about the need to replace the object in the way the group found it and why you are doing this. You might compare more than one "lift up" and think of reasons why you find the same kinds of creatures or different ones. Compare the plant life that is in the sun and out of the sun, under the board and talk about plants' need for sunlight.

Seed Walk

This is a fun activity for youngsters in summer or fall. You need a vacant lot or a grassy field and old socks that will fit over children's shoes. Tell them you are going on a discovery walk with your feet. Put on a sock over a shoe and walk through the field. You should gather all sorts of seeds that depend upon contact for dispersal.

Compare the sizes and shapes of what you have collected. Perhaps you can collect some of the seeds gathered and attempt to grow them in a pot at your meeting place. You can talk about what seeds are and how they travel. Find some seeds that depend upon wind travel, such as dandelions, and help them out with some deep breaths if they are ready to fly.

Eyes Plus

Gather an assortment of magnifying glasses, hand lenses, bug boxes, and at least one pair of binoculars. You can use these to enhance your nature walk or afterwards to look at non-living items gathered, such as leaves, rocks, feathers, or soil. Have the girls experiment with the distance their eyes or the object to be examined is from the lens. Have them look at something far away and then a bit closer with the binoculars. If possible, examine some insects on the hike with the hand lens and some squirrels or birds with the binoculars.

Shape Hike

Cut out a handful of shapes for each girl or pair of girls. They can be circles, squares, triangles, trapezoids, and other shapes of different sizes. Talk about the different shapes and how to tell them apart, then let the girls search to find shapes to match in nature. They can also look for patterns in nature, places where shapes are repeated again and again, such as in a beehive.

Mapping

Making maps is an excellent activity for Daisy Girl Scouts when they are learning about their neighborhoods and communities. The maps the girls make are special to their age and development.

They need to understand their environment in a very concrete way. Materials that are large and three-dimensional will help them to get a better understanding of how things work and exist in their communities. They need to be able to move within their maps and physically interact and play with them. Use large pieces of material, paper, and chalking on the floor to make rivers or streets. Boxes or blocks can be buildings, mountains, etc.

Wide Games

Wide games are trail-task games. Each game has a theme or story behind it, and everything done on the trail is connected to the story. Any place one can create a "trail" can be a place for a wide game—a neighborhood block, a room, the city, the country, a camp, the meeting place. Someone has to make up a story and then figure out a way to use the trail as part of the story. There may be stops along the trail called stations, where the players are asked to do various tasks connected with the wide game story. Usually, the person (or group) who makes up the story and the trail tasks does not play the game. She (or they) helps to guide players along and may help players understand the trail tasks.

As the trail tasks are completed, the girls get closer and closer to the end of the trail, where they find the answer, solve the mystery, or resolve the story. The girls can work as individuals, in pairs, or in groups.

The Story

A sample start for a wide game could be something like this:

"One day a Daisy Girl Scout lost her new puppy when she was walking him outside. He saw a bird and started to chase it, pulling the leash out of the girl's hand. The puppy kept running after the bird until he was out of the Daisy Girl Scout's sight. The girl was very upset, but she knew if she asked them, some of her Daisy Girl Scout friends would help her find her puppy.

"They got together and thought of all the places the puppy could have run after he was tired of chasing the bird. The first place they thought they should look was . . ."

122

The Tasks

The story then can be based on the particular place in which the girls are. At each station, they are asked to do certain things that connect to the story. These are figured out by the storymakers ahead of time (crawl under a fence, tie knots, sing a song, climb something, jump over something, feel, touch, or smell something). At the end of the trail, they should find the puppy (a willing volunteer in home-made doggy ears, or a picture, whatever).

Once the girls understand the basics of wide games, they can make up their own stories, trail tasks, stations, etc. Other ideas for wide games may be found in *Girl Scout Leader*, Spring 1983.

Camping

Family Camping

Daisy Girl Scouts can enjoy camping with their families at the council camp or an approved camping area. In planning the event, remember to include some opportunities for girl planning and girl/adult partnership. It is important to have parent meetings before the trip to explain the Girl Scout philosophy in regards to this, and to involve parents in the activity planning as well. See *Safety-Wise* and page 51 of this book under "Trips with Daisy Girl Scouts" for some additional information. Appropriate activities on a camping trip can be found in this and other world sections. Hiking, singing, meal preparation, nature crafts, and outdoor awareness activities can be a wonderful experience for a girl in an overnight camp setting with her parents/guardians.

Mom and Me

Many troops and/or councils have sponsored "mom and me" overnights at council-owned campsites. Girls can attend with mothers or guardians, grandmothers, or aunts. It is a special time to share activities with the woman role models in a girl's life. The same cautions and advice for activities apply to this type of overnight as for the family outings. Girls need opportunities to both share and experience activities of their own. They need to have a chance to show adults how to do activities as well as to learn from them.

Outdoor Cookery

Daisy Girl Scouts will not be in a position to cook by themselves over a campfire or a stove. However, they can help choose the menus and help in pre-cooking food preparation, if there is any. You may want to limit intake of sugars and rely on nutritious snacks, such as baked apple, apple with peanut butter, particularly at bedtime. Program time for girls and their parents is better spent out of the kitchen exploring nature and doing things they cannot do at home. Simple menus on overnights will be much easier for all involved.

Outdoor Action

Daisy Girl Scouts are old enough to understand the part of the Girl Scout Law that speaks to protecting and improving the environment around them. Girls can take pride in cleaning up an area after they have used it or by participating in a litter pick-up where they can see instant results of their actions. They can learn that they are a part of the world they live in and that their actions can affect that world in many ways. Simple nature walks can encourage discovery as well as appreciation for the out-of-doors. As a leader, you have access to many Girl Scout resources about the environment. It is suggested that you read the Contemporary Issues booklet on environmental action and *Exploring Wildlife Communities with Children*. The following are several outdoor action projects with which Daisy Girl Scouts might get involved.

Wildlife Habitat and Bird Feeders

Girls can make simple bird feeders by using fir or pine cones stuffed with suet (available at a butcher or meat market) and rolled in birdseed or corn meal. They can be hung outside a window and observed for the kinds of birds that are attracted. Be sure to hang any kind of bird feeder out of the reach of cats! In the winter, popcorn and cranberries strung on thread make a festive holiday treat for birds. Old trees piled in a backyard or empty lot can provide shelter and habitat for birds as well.

Willow trees can be planted along side streams and ponds for wildlife habitat improvement. You should be able to work with an agency that is interested in improving waterside habitats. They might assist by providing willow shoots and safe places to plant. Many states and communities have special Arbor Day activities and plantings in which youth groups can participate. Your group may also decide to plant a tree at a school or community park. Work with proper authorities in securing access and permission to plant on any public property. Be sure that the girls understand the responsibility they assume if they plant a tree. They may need to decide how to care for it or be involved in the arrangements with property managers for watering and fertilizing. Make plans to visit your tree periodically.

Litter Awareness and Pick-Up

A child is never too young to become aware of what littering does to the environment, and to formulate values that do not include littering as a daily practice. Picking up litter should become an automatic reflex when a group is on an outing. A spare bag should be part of a leader's equipment list on any trip outside. Girls and their families can become involved in community workdays or in picking up litter as a service project in the neighborhood or community park. Litter is something that is easy to measure for young people, and they should be able to draw some simple conclusions from the type of litter they see. They might ask why people litter, what are some of the solutions toward ending the problem. Litter can be introduced as a kind of pollution, and girls can talk about ways that they might prevent some kinds of pollution.

Recycling

If your community recycles glass, paper, or aluminum cans, involve girls in the process of recycling at the family and group level. If sodas are brought to group outings, make a point of having a special bag for recycling the cans or bottles. Make a game of collecting soda cans when on an outing and always have an extra plastic bag along when on nature walks. If possible, take girls to a recycling depot, so that they can see how items are sorted and sent on for processing.

Water Wasters

Young children can understand such concepts as drought and conservation if one puts them into terms that are relative to their daily experience. Hunger and poverty can be understood by daily visions of the poor and homeless. Lack of water can be shown by not watering a backyard plant. Saving water can be related to a daily action, such as taking a bath or brushing one's teeth. A graphic indoor or outdoor activity to show water waste can be done simply this way:

You will need a sink that can be stoppered or a plastic dish pan that fits into a sink. Provide a child with a toothbrush or have each girl bring her own. Have the child brush her teeth as she normally would, with the water running but not draining the sink. At the end, look at the amount of water used by one child to brush her teeth. Then have another child brush her teeth using a cup of water to dip her toothbrush in, wet her mouth with, and rinse with. Compare the amount of water used after this method. (It should only be the cup of water.) Talk about the amount of water wasted by the first method compared to the second method, and have the girls draw their own conclusions on which way would conserve more water.

126

Safety in the Out-of-Doors

". . .to respect authority. . ."
—Girl Scout Law

In the Girl Scout Law, Daisy Girl Scouts are encouraged to respect the authority of other people. Girls need to know that nature should also be respected as an authority.

By giving them appropriate information, you will help girls to learn as much as possible about the world of the out-of-doors and how they can safely experience it. Daisy Girl Scouts need not necessarily "love" all the plants and animals in nature. However, they need to appreciate the roles these animals and plants hold in the environment. Without making them overly fearful, help your girls understand about the things in nature that could cause them harm.

If you give them the right information, the girls will be able to enjoy the splendors of the natural world more safely and intelligently.

You and your Daisy Girl Scouts should be aware of poison ivy, poison sumac, poison oak, and any other poisonous plants, and of the animals in your area. It is also important to be able to identify those plants and animals in all seasons, as their appearances may change.

Find out if any of your troop members are allergic to particular plants or animals (bee stings, ragweed, grass, etc.), and take this into consideration when planning out-of-doors activities.

Safety-Wise should be your constant point of reference when out-of-doors activities are being planned. Also refer to "Working with Daisy Girl Scouts," pages 16 to 17.

Other Sources of Information

American Camping Association
5000 State Road, 67 N.
Martinsville, Ind. 46151

Appalachian Mountain Club
5 Joy Street
Boston, Mass. 02108

National Audubon Society
950 Third Avenue
New York, N.Y. 10022

National Wildlife Federation
1412 16th Street, N.W.
Washington, D.C. 20036

Outdoor Education Association
143 Fox Hill Road
Denville, N.J. 07834

Sierra Club
730 Polk Street
San Francisco, Calif. 94109

United States Fish and Wildlife Service
Washington, D.C. 20240

Wilderness Education Association
20 Winona Avenue
P.O. Box 89
North Country Community College
Saranac Lake, N.Y. 12983

Girl Scout Terms

Some of the following terms appear in this text. Others you will find in various Girl Scout materials.

adult: The age of majority, as defined by state statute.

Baden-Powell, Lord and Lady: Robert Baden-Powell was the founder of the Boy Scouts. Olave, his wife, was the World Chief Guide.

bridging: The move from one program age level of Girl Scouting to the next; for example, from Daisy Girl Scout to Brownie Girl Scout.

Brownie Girl Scout: A Girl Scout who is six through eight years old or in the first, second, or third grade.

Brownie Girl Scout pin: Trefoil-shaped pin with Brownie elf that signifies fulfillment of membership requirements.

Brownie Ring: A form of troop government used by Brownie Girl Scouts. It is a circle in which each girl shares in planning, problem-solving, and decision making with her troop.

buddy system: A safety practice in which girls of equal ability are paired, to help and to keep track of each other.

Cadette Girl Scout: A Girl Scout who is 11 through 14 years old or in the sixth, seventh, eighth, or ninth grade.

camp counselor: A staff member at a Girl Scout camp.

Campus Girl Scout: A Girl Scout who is 18 through 21 years old and belongs to a Campus Girl Scout group while attending college or working in a college community.

candlelight ceremony: An optional ceremony where candles are used for symbolic purposes. For example, three large and ten small candles may be lit to represent the parts of the Promise and Law.

color guard: The Girl Scouts who carry, guard, raise, and/or lower the flag or present the colors at a meeting or ceremony.

consultant: An adult whose knowledge and experience can aid Girl Scouts in the completion of an interest project or other Girl Scout activity.

council, Girl Scout: A corporation chartered by Girl Scouts of the U.S.A. and responsible for the development, management, and maintenance of Girl Scouting in a defined area (jurisdiction).

Daisy: The nickname of Juliette Gordon Low.

Daisy Girl Scout: A Girl Scout who is five or six years of age or in kindergarten or first grade.

Daisy Girl Scout circle: A form of government used by Daisy Girl Scouts that usually meets once a month.

The girls and their leader meet in a circle to plan, solve problems, and make decisions. It differs from the Brownie Ring in that the leader plays a more active role in structuring, directing, and decision making in Daisy Girl Scouting.

eco-action: The Girl Scout term for learning about the environment and taking care of it.

event: A wide-scale activity for Girl Scouts planned by a troop, council, or group of councils.

executive director: The chief executive officer in a Girl Scout council.

first aider (qualified): An adult who has completed and is currently certified in either the Standard First Aid and Personal Safety course or the Standard Multimedia course offered by the American Red Cross or a more advanced first aid and safety training certificate. This may include a physician, nurse (RN, LPN), physician's assistant, paramedic, emergency medical technician.

friendship circle: A symbolic gesture in which Girl Scouts form a circle by clasping each others' hands. It is often used as a closing ceremony.

fund raising: Techniques to appeal to the public for contributed funds to support the program and activities of the organization. Fund raising often relates to short-term needs and is only part of a fund development plan. Some fund-raising techniques include annual campaigns, capital campaigns, project funding, planned giving, and benefits. Fund raising to support the Girl Scout council is an adult responsibility.

Girl Guide: The original name for Girl Scouts, which is still used currently in many countries.

Girl Scout birthday: March 12 is the Girl Scout birthday, because it marks the first meeting of Girl Scouts in the U.S.A., in Savannah, Georgia, in 1912.

Girl Scout handshake: A formal way of greeting other Girl Scouts by shaking with the left hand, while giving the Girl Scout sign with the right.

Girl Scout insignia: All pins, patches, badges, or other recognitions worn on the Girl Scout uniform.

Girl Scout Leader: The official Girl Scout magazine sent to all registered adult members, and to Senior Girl Scouts who want to subscribe.

Girl Scout pins: Either of two pins—trefoil with three faces or trefoil with eagle—signifying fulfillment of membership requirements.

Girl Scout sign: The official Girl Scout greeting. The right hand is raised shoulder high with the three middle fingers extended and the thumb crossing over the palm to hold down the little finger.

Girl Scouts' Own: A quiet inspirational ceremony that has a theme and is planned by Girl Scouts and their leader.

Girl Scout Week: An annual celebration during the week of March 12, the Girl Scout birthday.

help for leaders: Those persons who are responsible for seeing that services are delivered to leaders and program to girls in the most direct and expeditious manner possible. They are known by a variety of names and titles. The most familiar are service team chairman, field manager, troop organizer, troop consultant, program consultant, field director, outdoor consultant, recruiter, trainer, public relations representative, competency team, community organization team.

investiture: A special ceremony in which a new member makes her Girl Scout Promise and receives her membership pin.

Junior Girl Scout: A Girl Scout who is 8 through 11 years old or in the third, fourth, fifth, or sixth grade.

kaper chart: A chart that shows the delegation of jobs and rotation of responsibility day by day, meal by meal, or meeting by meeting.

leader: An adult volunteer who meets regularly with a troop/group of Girl Scouts in town or in the out-of-doors.

motto: "Be prepared."

National Council: The membership body of the corporation, Girl Scouts of the U.S.A., in membership assembled. Membership consists of delegates elected by Girl Scout councils, the members of the National Board of Directors and the National Nominating Committee, and other persons elected by the National Council when assembled.

National Equipment Service (NES): GSUSA's service that sells uniforms, insignia, accessories, camping equipment, and printed materials used in Girl Scout program. Local NES agencies are located in licensed stores and in some Girl Scout offices.

neighborhood chairman (or service unit director): The adult volunteer chairman or head of a service team. The service team is responsible for organizing and delivering service to Girl Scout troops in a geographic subdivision within a council. Also called a service unit.

new games: A style of noncompetitive, safe, fair, fun, and interesting play that encourages total group participation.

outdoor day: A special outdoor event, planned and operated by a council, that provides staff, facilities, and site. Attendance is sometimes by troop, sometimes by individual girl members. The events may be carried out in neighborhood areas or may be councilwide or intercouncil in scope.

policy: An established course of action. Policies are binding on those whom they affect. The "Policies of Girl Scouts of the United States of America" are found in the *Blue Book of Basic Documents* and its *Leader's Digest*.

program consultant: A person who shares her or his interests and special abilities with troop members, usually by working directly with girls but sometimes by advising or instructing leaders or camp staff.

program emphases: Four interrelated areas of focus in Girl Scout program that together define what Girl Scouting strives to offer each girl. They are: developing self to achieve one's full individual potential; relating to others with increasing understanding, skill, and respect; developing values to guide her actions and to provide the foundation for sound decision-making; contributing to the improvement of society through her abilities and leadership skills, working in cooperation with others.

quiet sign: The Girl Scout signal for silence in a group situation. The person in charge raises her/his right hand, and the Girl Scouts present fall silent as they raise their right hands.

ranger: (1) A member of the maintenance staff at a Girl Scout camp. (2) *Cap.* The term for the oldest age grouping in some Girl Scout and Girl Guide associations in other countries.

recognition: An acknowledgement of accomplishments in Girl Scout program. It may be a pin, certificate, patch, badge, or letter.

Safety-Wise: A Girl Scout publication for Girl Scout adults that outlines safety principles and supplies safety references for specific Girl Scout activities in the form of program standards.

scribe: The troop secretary.

Senior Girl Scout: A Girl Scout who is 14 through 17 years old or in the ninth, tenth, eleventh, or twelfth grade.

service team: A group of adult volunteer workers who provide direct service to troops within a neighborhood or local geographic unit.

sister troop: A Brownie troop in the neighborhood or service unit that may receive Daisy Girl Scouts when they are ready to bridge to Brownies. A sister troop may also be a troop of any level with which friendship and activities such as parties, special occasions, joint service projects can be shared.

slogan: "Do a good turn daily."

standard: An established rule or principle intended to serve as a model or example.

trainer: A specially trained and certified person who gives leadership training at the council level.

trefoil: The international symbol of Girl Guiding and Girl Scouting. The three leaves of the trefoil represent the three parts of the Promise.

troop/group: The basic unit in Girl Scouting consisting of the girls and adult leader(s), and sometimes troop committee members.

troop/group consultant: A volunteer who provides ongoing help and advice to the troop/group leader. She or he is a member of the service team.

wide game: A game with a special purpose or theme that includes various tasks related to the theme.

wider opportunity: Any Girl Scout activity that takes girls outside their own troops and councils.

World Association pin: A pin with a gold trefoil on a blue field that may be worn by all Girl Scouts and Girl Guides. It is a symbol of the worldwide bond of Girl Scouting and Girl Guiding.

Daisy Girl Scout Story

The following may be read to or with Daisy Girl Scouts. It is the story of their namesake, Juliette "Daisy" Low.

Dear Daisy Girl Scout,

You are a Daisy Girl Scout and are named after "Daisy" Gordon Low. Daisy Low started Girl Scouts a long time ago in 1912. Her real name was Juliette, but most people called her "Daisy."

Juliette was born in 1860 on Halloween in a place called Savannah, Georgia. (Ask someone to show you where it is on a United States map.) Her uncle gave her the name "Daisy" when she was a baby. He looked at her one day and said, "I bet she's going to be a daisy!" He thought she was some baby! Ever since then people have called her Daisy.

Daisy had an older sister named Nellie and four younger sisters and brothers—named Alice, Willy, Mabel, and Arthur. Her father was a cotton trader, and her mother was a homemaker, busy taking care of all the children, the family, and their house.

They lived in a big house in Savannah. (Now it is a Girl Scout program center, and if you are ever in Savannah, Georgia, you can visit the Juliette Gordon Low Birthplace on 142 Bull Street, Savannah, Georgia.)

132

133

Daisy's father and grandmother knew that she loved animals, especially horses. When they thought she was old enough to take care of one, they bought her a horse. She named the horse Fire and spent many hours riding him, grooming him, and talking to him. He was black with four white feet. Daisy was very, very happy to have a horse and took very good care of him.

As a young girl, Daisy did many things. She liked to climb trees, play with her brothers, sisters, and cousins, take care of animals, start and run clubs, write stories, draw pictures, tell jokes, write and be in plays, explore places, and do many other things.

One time she saved a kitten from being drowned in a flood. Another time she kept a cow from getting really sick by putting her mother's blanket on the cow overnight. Her mother did not like that too much, because the blanket fell off the cow in the morning and the cow stepped on it. But at least the cow did not get sick.

Later on, Daisy grew up and married a man named Willy Low. They went to live in England and Scotland, countries on the other side of the Atlantic Ocean. (Ask someone to show you on a world map where they are.)

They lived together for many years, but then Willy died. Other sad things had happened to Daisy, too. She had problems with her ears and became partially deaf.

Even with these sad events in her life, she went on to do many wonderful things. She heard about Boy Scouts and Girl Guides from her friend Lord Robert Baden-Powell. Daisy decided to start the same thing for girls in the United States. After leading a few troops of Girl Guides in Scotland, she came back to the United States and started Girl Scouts. On March 12, 1912, the first troop met. That's why March 12 is the Girl Scout birthday.

Very soon Girl Scouting was happening in different parts of the country. Girls 10 years old and older were helping others, making friends, camping, deciding on things, planning, learning, working and playing together. (Now girls from Daisy Girl Scouts to Senior Girl Scouts can enjoy Girl Scouting.) And Daisy made sure that Girl Scouts in the United States were sisters to all the Girl Guides and Girl Scouts in other parts of the world.

Daisy died a long time ago in 1927. She lived to be almost 67 years old. She did many things in her life. Daisy had fun, helped other people, loved animals, and started Girl Scouts in the United States. Her uncle was right! She sure was a DAISY! And so are YOU!

Index

Program 11/83, rev. 6/89